Richard Hakluyt

Voyager's Tales

From the Collections of Richard Hakluyt

Richard Hakluyt

Voyager's Tales
From the Collections of Richard Hakluyt

ISBN/EAN: 9783337070779

Printed in Europe, USA, Canada, Australia, Japan

Cover: Foto ©ninafisch / pixelio.de

More available books at **www.hansebooks.com**

CASSELL'S NATIONAL LIBRARY.

VOYAGERS' TALES

FROM THE COLLECTIONS OF

RICHARD HAKLUYT.

CASSELL & COMPANY, Limited:

LONDON, PARIS, NEW YORK & MELBOURNE.

1886.

INTRODUCTION.

RICHARD HAKLUYT, notwithstanding the Dutch look of his name, was of a good British stock, from Wales or the Welsh borders. At the beginning of the fourteenth century an ancestor of his, Hugo Hakelute, sat in Parliament as member for Leominster.

Richard Hakluyt, born about five years before the accession of Queen Elizabeth, was a boy at Westminster School, when visits to a cousin in the Middle Temple, also a Richard Hakluyt, first planted in him an enthusiasm for the study of adventure towards a wider use and knowledge of the globe we live upon. As a student at Christ Church, Oxford, all his leisure was spent on the collection and reading of accounts of voyage and adventure. He graduated as B.A. in 1574, as M.A. in 1577, and lectured publicly upon geography, showing "both the old imperfectly composed, and the new lately reformed maps, globes, spheres, and other instruments of this art."

In 1582 Hakluyt, at the age of about twenty-nine, issued his first publication: "Divers Voyages touching the Discovery of America and the Lands adjacent unto the same, made first of all by our Englishmen, and afterwards by the Frenchmen and Bretons: and certain Notes of Advertisements for Observations, necessary for such as shall hereafter make the like Attempt." His researches had already made him the personal friend of the famous sea captains of Elizabeth's reign. In 1583 he had taken orders, and went to Paris as chaplain to the English ambassador, Sir Edward Stafford. From Paris he returned to England for a short time, in 1584, and laid before the Queen a paper recommending the plantation of unsettled parts of America. It was called "A particular Discourse concerning Western Discoveries, written in the year 1584, by Richard Hakluyt, of Oxford, at the request and direction of the right worshipful Mr. Walter Raleigh, before the coming home of his two barks." Raleigh and Hakluyt were within a year of the same age.

To found a colonial empire in America by settling upon new lands, and by dispossessing Spaniards, was one of the grand ideas of Walter Raleigh, who obtained, on the 25th of March in that year, 1584, a patent authorising him to search out and take possession of new lands in the Western world. He then fitted out two ships, which left England on the 27th of April, under the command of Philip Amadas and Arthur Barlow. In June they had reached the West Indies, then they sailed north by the coasts of Florida and Carolina, and they had with them two natives when they returned to England in September, 1584. In December Raleigh's patent was enlarged and confirmed, and presently afterwards Raleigh was knighted.

Richard Hakluyt's paper, in aid of this beginning of the shaping of another England in the New World, was for a long time lost. It was first printed in 1877 at Cambridge, Massachusetts, among the Collections of the Maine Historical Society. It won for its author a promise of the next vacant prebend at Bristol; the vacancy came about a year later, and the Rev. Richard Hakluyt was admitted to it in 1586.

Hakluyt remained about five years at Paris as Chaplain to the English Embassy, and while there he caused the publication in 1586 of an account by Laudonnière of voyages into Florida. This he also translated and published, in London, in 1587, as "A Notable History containing Four Voyages made by certain French Captains into Florida." In 1588 Hakluyt returned to England, and in the next year, 1589, he published in one folio volume, "The Principal Navigations, Voyages, and Discoveries of the English Nation." In April of the next year he became rector of Witheringsett-cum-Brockford, in Suffolk. The full development of his work appeared in three volumes folio in the years 1598, 1599, and 1600, as "The Principal Navigations, Voyages, Traffics, and Discoveries of the English Nation," the first of these volumes differing materially from the volume that had appeared in 1589.

Hakluyt became, in May, 1602, prebendary, and in 1603 archdeacon of Westminster. He was twice married, died about six months after Shakespeare, and was buried in Westminster Abbey on the 26th of November, 1616.

H. M.

VOYAGERS' TALES.

THE WORTHY ENTERPRISE OF JOHN FOX,

An Englishman, in delivering 266 Christians out of the captivity of the Turks at Alexandria, the 3rd of January, 1577.

AMONG our merchants here in England, it is a common voyage to traffic to Spain; whereunto a ship called the *Three Half Moons*, manned with eight and thirty men, well fenced with munitions, the better to encounter their enemies withal, and having wind and tide, set from Portsmouth 1563, and bended her journey towards Seville, a city in Spain, intending there to traffic with them. And falling near the Straits, they perceived themselves to be beset round about with eight galleys of the Turks, in such wise that there was no way for them to fly or to escape away, but that either they must yield or else be sunk, which the owner perceiving, manfully encouraged his company, exhorting them valiantly to show their manhood, showing them that God was their God, and not their enemies', requesting them also not to faint in seeing such a heap of their enemies ready to devour them; putting them in mind also, that if it were God's pleasure to give them into their enemies' hands, it was not they that ought to show one displeasant look or countenance there against; but to take it patiently, and not to prescribe a day and time for their deliverance, as the citizens of Bethulia did, but to put themselves under His mercy. And again, if it were His mind and good will to show His mighty power by them, if their enemies were ten times so many, they were not able to stand in their hands; putting them, likewise, in mind of the old and ancient worthiness of their countrymen, who in the hardest extremities have always most prevailed, and gone away conquerors; yea, and where it hath been almost impossible. "Such," quoth he, "hath been the valiantness of our countrymen, and such hath been the mighty power of our God."

With such other like encouragements, exhorting them to behave themselves manfully, they fell all on their knees, making their prayers briefly unto God; who, being all risen up again, perceived their enemies, by their signs and defiances, bent to the spoil, whose mercy was nothing else but cruelty; whereupon every man took him to his weapon.

Then stood up one Grove, the master, being a comely man, with his sword and target, holding them up in defiance against his enemies. So likewise stood up the owner, the master's mate, boatswain, purser, and every man well appointed. Now likewise sounded up the drums, trumpets, and flutes, which would have encouraged any man, had he never so little heart or courage in him.

Then taketh him to his charge John Fox, the gunner, in the disposing of his pieces, in order to the best effect, and, sending his bullets towards the Turks, who likewise bestowed their pieces thrice as fast towards the Christians. But shortly they drew near, so that the bowmen fell to their charge in sending forth their arrows so thick amongst the galleys, and also in doubling their shot so sore upon the galleys, that there were twice so many of the Turks slain as the number of the Christians were in all. But the Turks discharged twice as fast against the Christians, and so long, that the ship was very sore stricken and bruised under water; which the Turks, perceiving, made the more haste to come aboard the ship: which, ere they could do, many a Turk bought it dearly with the loss of their lives. Yet was all in vain, boarded they were, where they found so hot a skirmish, that it had been better they had not meddled with the feast; for the Englishmen showed themselves men indeed, in working manfully with their brown bills and halberds, where the owner, master, boatswain, and their company stood to it so lustily, that the Turks were half dismayed. But chiefly the boatswain showed himself valiant above the rest, for he fared amongst the Turks like a wood lion; for there was none of them that either could or durst stand in his face, till at last there came a shot from the Turks which brake his whistle asunder, and smote him on the breast, so that he fell down, bidding them farewell, and to be of good comfort, encouraging them, likewise, to win praise by death, rather than to live captives in misery and shame, which they, hearing, indeed, intended to have done, as it appeared by their skirmish; but the press and store of the Turks were so great, that they were not long able to endure, but were so overpressed, that they could not wield their weapons, by reason whereof they must needs be taken, which none of them intended to have been, but rather to have died, except only the master's mate, who shrunk from the skirmish, like a notable coward, esteeming neither the value of his name, nor accounting of the present example of his fellows, nor having respect to the miseries whereunto he should be put. But in fine, so it was, that the Turks were victors, whereof they had no great cause to rejoice or triumph. Then would it have grieved any hard heart to see these infidels so violently entreating the Christians, not having any respect of their manhood, which they had tasted of, nor yet respecting their own state, how they might have met with such a booty as might have given them the overthrow; but no remorse hereof, or anything else doth bridle their fierce and tyrannous dealing, but the Christians must needs to the galleys, to serve in new offices; and they were no sooner in them, but their garments were pulled over their ears, and torn from their backs, and they set to the oars.

I will make no mention of their miseries, being now under their enemies' raging stripes. I think there is no man will judge their fare good, or their bodies unloaden of stripes, and not pestered with too much heat, and also with too much cold; but I will go to my purpose, which is to show the end of those being in mere misery, which continually do call on God with a steadfast hope that He will deliver them, and with a sure faith that He can do it.

Nigh to the city of Alexandria, being a haven

town, and under the dominion of the Turks, there is a road, being made very fencible with strong walls, whereinto the Turks do customably bring their galleys on shore every year, in the winter season, and there do trim them, and lay them up against the spring-time; in which road there is a prison, wherein the captives and such prisoners as serve in the galleys are put for all that time, until the seas be calm and passable for the galleys, every prisoner being most grievously laden with irons on their legs, to their great pain, and sore disabling of them to any labour; into which prison were these Christians put and fast warded all the winter season. But ere it was long, the master and the owner, by means of friends, were redeemed, the rest abiding still in the misery, while that they were all, through reason of their ill-usage and worse fare, miserably starved, saving one John Fox, who (as some men can abide harder and more misery than other some can, so can some likewise make more shift, and work more duties to help their state and living, than other some can do) being somewhat skilful in the craft of a barber, by reason thereof made great shift in helping his fare now and then with a good meal. Insomuch, till at the last God sent him favour in the sight of the keeper of the prison, so that he had leave to go in and out to the road at his pleasure, paying a certain stipend, unto the keeper, and wearing a lock about his leg, which liberty likewise five more had upon like sufferance, who, by reason of their long imprisonment, not being feared or suspected to start aside, or that they would work the Turks any mischief, had liberty to go in and out at the said road, in such manner as this John Fox did, with irons on their legs, and to return again at night.

In the year of our Lord 1577, in the winter season, the galleys happily coming to their accustomed harbourage, and being discharged of all their masts, sails, and other such furnitures as unto galleys do appertain, and all the masters and mariners of them being then nested in their own homes, there remained in the prison of the said road two hundred three score and eight Christian prisoners who had been taken by the Turks' force, and were of fifteen sundry nations. Among which there were three Englishmen, whereof one was named John Fox, of Woodbridge, in Suffolk, the other William Wickney, of Portsmouth, in the county of Southampton, and the third Robert Moore, of Harwich, in the county of Essex; which John Fox, having been thirteen or fourteen years under their gentle entreatance, and being too weary thereof, minding his escape, weighed with himself by what means it might be brought to pass, and continually pondering with himself thereof, took a good heart unto him, in the hope that God would not be always scourging His children, and never ceasing to pray Him to further his intended enterprise, if that it should redound to His glory.

Not far from the road, and somewhat from thence, at one side of the city, there was a certain victualling house, which one Peter Vuticaro had hired, paying also a certain fee unto the keeper of the road. This Peter Vuticaro was a Spaniard born, and a Christian, and had been prisoner above thirty years, and never practised any means to escape, but kept himself quiet without touch or suspect of any conspiracy, until that now this John Fox using much thither, they brake one to another their minds, concerning the restraint of their liberty and imprisonment. So that this John Fox, at length opening unto this Vuticaro the device which he would fain put in practice, made privy one more to this their intent; which three debated of this matter at such times as they could compass to meet together, insomuch that, at seven weeks' end they had sufficiently concluded how the matter should be, if it pleased God to further them thereto; who, making five more privy to this their device, whom they thought that they might safely trust, determined in three nights after to accomplish their deliberate purpose. Whereupon the same John Fox and Peter Vuticaro, and the other five appointed to meet all together in the prison the next day, being the last day of December, where this John Fox certified the rest of the prisoners what their intent and device was, and how and when they minded to bring that purpose to pass, who thereunto persuaded them without much ado to further their device; which, the same John Fox seeing, delivered unto them a sort of files, which he had gathered together for this purpose by the means of Peter Vuticaro, charging them that every man should be ready, discharged of his irons, by eight of the clock on the next day at night.

On the next day at night, the said John Fox, and his five other companions, being all come to the house of Peter Vuticaro, passing the time away in mirth for fear of suspect till the night came on, so that it was time for them to put in practice their device, sent Peter Vuticaro to the master of the road, in the name of one of the masters of the city, with whom this keeper was acquainted, and at whose request he also would come at the first; who desired him to take the pains to meet him there, promising him that he would bring him back again. The keeper agreed to go with him, asking the warders not to bar the gate, saying that he would not stay long, but would come again with all speed.

In the mean-season, the other seven had provided them of such weapons as they could get in that house, and John Fox took him to an old rusty sword-blade without either hilt or pommel, which he made to serve his turn in bending the hand end of the sword instead of a pommel, and the other had got such spits and glaves as they found in the house.

The keeper being now come unto the house, and perceiving no light nor hearing any noise, straightway suspected the matter; and returning backward, John Fox, standing behind the corner of the house, stepped forth unto him; who, perceiving it to be John Fox, said, "O Fox, what have I deserved of thee that thou shouldest seek my death?" "Thou villain," quoth Fox, "hast been a bloodsucker of many a Christian's blood, and now thou shalt know what thou hast deserved at my hands," wherewith he lift up his bright shining sword of ten years' rust, and stroke him so main a blow, as therewithal his head clave asunder so that he fell stark dead to the ground. Whereupon Peter Vuticaro went in and certified the rest how the case stood with the keeper, and they came presently forth, and some with their spits ran him through, and the other with their glaves hewed him in sunder, cut off his head, and mangled him so that no man should discern what he was.

Then marched they toward the road, whereinto they entered softly, where were five warders, whom one of them asked, saying, who was there? Quoth Fox and his company, "All friends." Which when they were all within proved contrary; for, quoth Fox, "My masters, here is not to every man a man, wherefore look you, play your parts." Who so behaved themselves indeed, that they had despatched these five quickly. Then John Fox, intending not to be barren of his enterprise, and minding to work surely in that which he went about, barred the gate surely, and planted a cannon against it.

Then entered they into the jailer's lodge, where they found the keys of the fortress and prison by his bedside, and there got they all better weapons. In this chamber was a chest wherein was a rich treasure, and all in ducats, which this Peter Vuticaro and two more opening, stuffed themselves so full as they could between their shirts and their skin; which John Fox would not once touch, and said, "that it was his and their liberty which he fought for, to the honour of his God, and not to make a mart of the wicked treasure of the infidels." Yet did these words sink nothing unto their stomachs; they did it for a good intent. So did Saul save the fattest oxen to offer unto the Lord, and they to serve their own turn. But neither did Saul scape the wrath of God therefor, neither had these that thing which they desired so, and did thirst after. Such is God's justice. He that they put their trust in to deliver them from the tyrannous hands of their enemies, he, I say, could supply their want of necessaries.

Now these eight, being armed with such weapons as they thought well of, thinking themselves sufficient champions to encounter a stronger enemy, and coming unto the prison, Fox opened the gates and doors thereof, and called forth all the prisoners, whom he set, some to ramming up the gate, some to the dressing up of a certain galley which was the best in all the road, and was called "The Captain of Alexandria," whereinto some carried masts, sails, oars, and other such furniture, as doth belong unto a galley.

At the prison were certain warders whom John Fox and his company slew, in the killing of whom there were eight more of the Turks which perceived them, and got them to the top of the prison, unto whom John Fox and his company were fain to come by ladders, where they found a hot skirmish, for some of them were there slain, some wounded, and some but scarred and not hurt. As John Fox was thrice shot through his apparel, and not hurt, Peter Vuticaro and the other two, that had armed them with the ducats, were slain, as not able to wield themselves, being so pestered with the weight and uneasy carrying of the wicked and profane treasure; and also divers Christians were as well hurt about that skirmish as Turks slain.

Amongst the Turks was one thrust through, who (let us not say that it was ill-fortune) fell off from the top of the prison wall, and made such a groaning that the inhabitants thereabout (as here and there stood a house or two), came and questioned him, so that they understood the case, how that the prisoners were paying their ransoms; wherewith they raised both Alexandria, which lay on the west side of the road, and a castle which was at the city's end next to the road, and also another fortress which lay on the north side of the road, so that now they had no way to escape but one, which by man's reason (the two holds lying so upon the mouth of the road) might seem impossible to be a way for them. So was the Red Sea impossible for the Israelites to pass through, the hills and rocks lay so on the one side, and their enemies compassed them on the other. So was it impossible that the walls of Jericho should fall down, being neither undermined nor yet rammed at with engines, nor yet any man's wisdom, policy, or help, set or put thereunto. Such impossibilities can our God make possible. He that held the lion's jaws from rending Daniel asunder, yea, or yet from once touching him to his hurt, cannot He hold the roaring cannons of this hellish force? He that kept the fire's rage in the hot burning oven from the three children that praised His name, cannot He keep the fire's flaming blasts from among His elect?

Now is the road fraught with lusty soldiers, labourers, and mariners, who are fain to stand to their tackling, in setting to every man his hand, some to the carrying in of victuals, some munitions, some oars, and some one thing some another, but most are keeping their enemy from the wall of the road. But to be short, there was no time misspent, no man idle, nor any man's labour illbestowed or in vain. So that in short time this galley was ready trimmed up. Whereinto every man leaped in all haste, hoisting up the sails lustily, yielding themselves to His mercy and grace, in Whose hands is both wind and weather.

Now is this galley a-float, and out of the shelter of the road; now have the two castles full power upon the galley; now is there no remedy but to sink. How can it be avoided? The cannons let fly from both sides, and the galley is even in the middest and between them both. What man can devise to save it? There is no man but would think it must needs be sunk.

There was not one of them that feared the shot which went thundering round about their ears, nor yet were once scarred or touched with five and forty shot which came from the castles. Here did God hold forth His buckler, He shieldeth now this galley, and hath tried their faith to the uttermost. Now cometh His special help; yea, even when man thinks them past all help, then cometh He Himself down from Heaven with His mighty power, then is His present remedy most ready. For they sail away, being not once touched by the glance of a shot, and are quickly out of the Turkish cannons' reach. Then might they see them coming down by heaps to the water's side, in companies like unto swarms of bees, making show to come after them with galleys, bustling themselves to dress up the galleys, which would be a swift piece of work for them to do, for that they had neither oars, masts, sails, nor anything else ready in any galley. But yet they are carrying into them, some into one galley, and some into another, so that, being such a confusion amongst them, without any certain guide, it were a thing impossible to overtake the Christians; beside that, there was no man that would take charge of a galley, the weather was so rough, and there was such an amazedness amongst them. And verily, I think their god was amazed thereat; it could not be but that he must blush for shame, he can speak never a word for dulness, much less can he help them in such an extremity. Well, howsoever it is, he is very much to blame to suffer them to receive such a gibe. But howsoever their god behaved himself, our God showed Himself a God indeed, and that He was the only living God; for the seas were swift under His faithful, which made the enemies aghast to behold them; a skilfuller pilot leads them, and their mariners bestir them lustily; but the Turks had neither mariners, pilot, nor any skilful master, that was in readiness at this pinch.

When the Christians were safe out of the enemy's coast, John Fox called to them all, telling them to be thankful unto Almighty God for their delivery, and most humbly to fall down upon their knees, beseeching Him to aid them to their friends' land, and not to bring them into another danger, since He had most mightily delivered them from so great a thraldom and bondage.

Thus when every man had made his petition, they fell straightway to their labour with the oars, in helping one another when they were wearied, and with great labour striving to come to some Christian land, as near as they could guess by the stars. But the winds were so contrary, one while driving them this way, another while that way, so that they were now in a new maze, thinking that God had forsaken them and left them to a greater danger. And forasmuch as there were no victuals now left in the galley, it might have been a cause to them (if they had been the Israelites), to have murmured against their God; but they knew how that their God, who had delivered Egypt, was such a loving and merciful God, as that He would not suffer them to be confounded in whom He had wrought so great a wonder, but what calamity soever they sustained, they knew it was but for their further trial, and also (in putting them in mind of their further misery), to cause them not to triumph and glory in themselves therefor. Having, I say, no victuals in the galley, it might seem one misery continually to fall upon another's neck; but to be brief the famine grew to be so great that in twenty-eight days, wherein they were on the sea, there died eight persons, to the astonishment of all the rest.

So it fell out that upon the twenty-ninth day after they set from Alexandria, they fell on the isle of Candia, and landed at Gallipoli, where they were made much of by the abbot and monks there, who caused them to stay there while they were well refreshed and eased. They kept there the sword wherewith John Fox had killed the keeper, esteeming it as a most precious relic, and hung it up for a monument.

When they thought good, having leave to depart from thence, they sailed along the coast till they arrived at Tarento, where they sold their galley, and divided it, every man having a part thereof. The Turks on receiving so shameful a foil at their hands, pursued the Christians, and scoured the seas, where they could imagine that they had bent their course. And the Christians had departed from thence on the one day in the morning and seven galleys of the Turks came thither that night, as it was certified by those who followed Fox and his company, fearing lest they should have been met with. And then they came afoot to Naples, where they departed asunder, every man taking him to his next way home. From whence John Fox took his journey unto Rome, where he was well entertained by an Englishman who presented his worthy deed unto the Pope, who rewarded him liberally, and gave him letters unto the King of Spain, where he was very well entertained of him there, who for this his most worthy enterprise gave him in fee twenty pence a day. From whence, being desirous to come into his own country, he came thither at such time as he conveniently could, which was in the year of our Lord God 1579; who being come into England went unto the Court, and showed all his travel unto the Council, who considering of the state of this man, in that he had spent and lost a great part of his youth in thraldom and bondage, extended to him their liberality to help to maintain him now in age, to their right honour and to the encouragement of all true-hearted Christians.

The copy of the certificate for John Fox and his Company, made by the Prior and the Brethren of Gallipoli, where they first landed.

We, the Prior and Fathers of the Convent of the Amerciates, of the city of Gallipoli, of the order of Preachers, do testify that upon the 29th of January last past, 1577, there came into the said city a certain galley from Alexandria, taken from the Turks, with two hundred and fifty-eight

Christians, whereof was principal Master John Fox, an Englishman, a gunner, and one of the chiefest that did accomplish that great work, whereby so many Christians have recovered their liberties, in token and remembrance whereof, upon our earnest request to the same John Fox, he has left here an old sword, wherewith he slew the keeper of the prison, which sword we do as a monument and memorial of so worthy a deed, hang up in the chief place of our convent house. And for because all things aforesaid, are such as we will testify to be true, as they are orderly passed, and have therefore good credit, that so much as is above expressed is true, and for the more faith thereof, we, the Prior and Fathers aforesaid, have ratified and subscribed these presents. Given in Gallipoli, the 3rd of February, 1577.

> I, Friar VINCENT BARBA, Prior of the same place, confirm the premises, as they are above written.
>
> I, Friar ALBERT DAMARO, of Gallipoli, sub-prior, confirm as much.
>
> I, Friar ANTHONY CELLELER, of Galli, confirm as aforesaid.
>
> I, Friar BARTLEMEW, of Gallipoli, confirm as above said.
>
> I, Friar FRANCIS, of Gallipoli, confirm as much.

The Bishop of Rome, his letters in behalf of John Fox.

Be it known unto all men, to whom this writing shall come, that the bringer hereof, John Fox, Englishman, a gunner, after he had served captive in the Turks' galleys, by the space of fourteen years, at length, through God his help, taking good opportunity, the 3rd of January last passed, slew the keeper of the prison (whom he first stroke on the face) together with four and twenty other Turks, by the assistance of his fellow-prisoners; and with 266 Christians (of whose liberty he was the author) launched from Alexandria, and from thence arrived first at Gallipoli, in Candia, and afterwards at Tarento, in Apulia; the written testimony and credit of which things, as also of others, the same John Fox hath in public tables from Naples.

Upon Easter Eve he came to Rome, and is now determined to take his journey to the Spanish Court, hoping there to obtain some relief towards his living; wherefore the poor distressed man humbly beseecheth, and we in his behalf, do in the bowels of Christ, desire you, that taking compassion of his former captivity and present penury, you do not only suffer him freely to pass through all your cities and towns, but also succour him with your charitable alms, the reward whereof you shall hereafter most assuredly receive, which we hope you will afford to him, whom with tender affection of pity we commend unto you. At Rome, the 20th of April, 1577.

> THOMAS GROLOS, Englishman, Bishop of Astraphen.
>
> RICHARD SILLEUN, Prior Angliæ.
>
> ANDREAS LUDOVICUS, Register to our Sovereign Lord the Pope, which for the greater credit of the premises, have set my seal to these presents. At Rome, the day and year above written.
>
> MAURICIUS CLEMENT, the governor and keeper of the English hospital in the city.

The King of Spain, his letters to the Lieutenant for the placing of John Fox in the office of a gunner, &c.

To the illustrious prince, Vespasian Gonsaga Colonna, our Lieutenant and Captain-General of our realm of Valencia, having consideration that John Fox, Englishman, hath served us, and was one of the most principal which took away from the Turks a certain galley, which they have brought to Taranto, wherein were two hundred and fifty-eight Christian captives. We license him to practice, and give him the office of a gunner, and have ordained that he go to our said realm there to serve in the said office in the galleys, which by our commandment are lately made. And we do command that you cause to be paid to him eight ducats pay a month, for the time that he shall serve in the said galleys as a gunner, or till we can otherwise provide for him, the said eight ducats monthly of the money which is already of our provision, present and to come, and to have regard of those which come with him. From Escurial the 10th of August, 1577.—I, the King,

JUAN DEL GADO.

And under that a confirmation of the Council.

Verses written by A. M. to the courteous readers, who was present at Rome when John Fox received his letters of the Pope.

Leaving at large all fables vainly used,
All trifling toys that do no truth import,
Lo, here how the end (at length) though long diffused,
Unfoldeth plain a true and rare report;
To glad those minds which seek their country's wealth,
By proffered pains to enlarge his happy health.
At Rome I was, when Fox did there arrive,
Therefore I may sufficiently express,
What gallant joy his deeds did there revive

In the hearts of those which heard his valiantness.
And how the Pope did recompense his pains,
And letters gave to move his greater gains.

But yet I know that many do misdoubt,
That those his pains are fables and untrue;
Not only I in this will bear him out,
But diverse more that did his patents view,
And unto those so boldly I daresay,
That nought but truth John Fox doth here bewray.
Besides here's one was slave with him in thrall,
Lately returned into our native land,
This witness can this matter perfect all,
What needeth more? for witness he may stand.
And thus I end, unfolding what I know,
The other man more larger proof can show.

Honos alit artes,   A. M.

THE VOYAGE MADE TO TRIPOLIS IN BARBARY,

In the Year 1584, *with a ship called the* JESUS, *wherein the adventures and distresses of some Englishmen are truly reported, and other necessary circumstances observed. Written by* THOMAS SANDERS.

THIS voyage was set forth by the Right Worshipful Sir Edward Osborne Knight, chief merchant of all the Turkish Company, and one Master

Richard Stapers, the ship being of the burden of one hundred tons, called the *Jesus;* she was builded at Farmne, a river by Portsmouth. The owners were Master Thomas Thompson, Nicholas Carnabie, and John Gilman. The master (under God) was one Zaccheus Hellier, of Blackwall, and his mate was one Richard Morris, of that place; their pilot was one Anthony Jerado, a Frenchman, of the province of Marseilles; the purser was one William Thompson, our owner's son; the merchants' factors were Romane Sonnings, a Frenchman, and Richard Skegs, servant unto the said Master Stapers. The owners were bound unto the merchants by charter party thereupon in one thousand marks, that the said ship, by God's permission should go for Tripolis in Barbary, that is to say, first from Portsmouth to Newhaven in Normandy, thence to S. Lukar, otherwise called S. Lucas, in Andalusia, and from thence to Tripolis, which is in the east part of Africa, and so to return unto London.

But here ought every man to note and consider the works of our God, that (many times) what man doth determine God doth disappoint. The said master having some occasion to go to Farmne, took with him the pilot and the purser, and returning again, by means of a gust of wind, the boat wherein they were was drowned, the said master, the purser, and all the company; only the said pilot by experience in swimming saved himself, these were the beginnings of our sorrows. After which the said master's mate would not proceed in that voyage, and the owner hearing of this misfortune, and the unwillingness of the master's mate, did send down one Richard Deimond and shipped him for master, who did choose for his mate one Andrew Dier, and so the said ship departed on her voyage accordingly; that is to say, about the 16th of October, 1584, she made sail from Portsmouth, and the 18th day then next following she arrived into Newhaven, where our said last master Deimond by a surfeit died. The factors then appointed the said Andrew Dier, being then master's mate, to be their master for that voyage, who did choose to be his mates the two quarter-masters of the same ship, to wit, Peter Austine and Shillabey, and for purser was shipped one Richard Burges. Afterward about the 8th day of November we made sail forthward, and by force of weather we were driven back again into Portsmouth, where we refreshed our victuals and other necessaries, and then the wind came fair. About the 29th day then next following we departed thence, and the 1st day of December, by means of a contrary wind, we were driven to Plymouth. The 18th day then next following we made forthward again, and by force of weather we were driven to Falmouth, where we remained until the 1st day of January, at which time the wind coming fair we departed thence, and about the 20th day of the said month we arrived safely at S. Lucas. And about the 9th day of March next following we made sail from thence, and about the 18th day of the same month we came to Tripolis in Barbary, where we were very well entertained by the king of that country and also of the commons. The commodities of that place are sweet oils; the king there is a merchant, and the rather (willing to prefer himself before his commons) requested our said factors to traffic with him, and promised them that if they would take his oils at his own price they should pay no manner of custom, and they took of him certain tons of oil; and afterward perceiving that they might have far better cheap, notwithstanding the custom free, they desired the king to license them to take the oils at the pleasure of his commons, for that his price did exceed theirs; whereunto the king would not agree, but was rather contented to abate his price, insomuch that the factors bought all their oils of the king's custom free, and so laded the same aboard.

In the meantime there came to that place one Miles Dickinson, in a ship of Bristol, who together with our said factors took a house to themselves there. Our French factor, Romaine Sonnings, desired to buy a commodity in the market, and, wanting money, desired the said Miles Dickinson to lend him a hundred chikinoes until he came to his lodging, which he did; and afterwards the same Sonnings met with Miles Dickinson in the street, and delivered him money bound up in a napkin, saying, "Master Dickinson, there is the money that I borrowed of you," and so thanked him for the same. He doubted nothing less than falsehood, which is seldom known among merchants, and specially being together in one house, and is the more detestable between Christians, they being in Turkey among the heathen; the said Dickinson did not tell the money presently, until he came to his lodging, and then, finding nine chikinoes lacking of his hundred (which was about three pounds, for that every chikinoe is worth seven shillings of English money), he came to the said Romaine Sonnings and delivered him his handkerchief, and asked him how many chikinoes he had delivered him. Sonnings answered, "A hundred"; Dickinson said "No"; and so they protested and swore on both parts. But in the end the said Romaine Sonnings did swear deeply with detestable oaths and curses, and prayed God that he might show his works on him, that other might take ensample thereby, and that he might be hanged like a dog, and never come into England again, if he did not deliver unto the said Dickinson a hundred chikinoes. And here behold a notable example of all blasphemers, cursers, and swearers, how God rewarded him accordingly; for many times it cometh to pass that God showeth his miracles upon such monstrous blasphemers to the ensample of others, as now hereafter you shall hear what befell to this Romaine Sonnings.

There was a man in the said town a pledge, whose name was Patrone Norado, who the year before had done this Sonnings some pleasure there. The foresaid Patrone Norado was indebted unto a Turk of that town in the sum of four hundred and fifty crowns, for certain goods sent by him into Christendom in a ship of his own, and by his own brother, and himself remained in Tripolis as pledge until his said brother's return; and, as the report went there, he came among lewd company, and lost his brother's said ship and goods at dice, and never returned unto him again.

The said Patrone Norado, being void of all hope and finding now opportunity, consulted with the said Sonnings for to swim a-seaboard the islands, and the ship, being then out of danger, should take him in (as was afterwards confessed), and so go to Tallowne, in the province of Marseilles, with this Patrone Norado, and there to take in the rest of his lading.

The ship being ready the first day of May, and having her sails all abroad, our said factors did take their leave of the king, who very courteously bid them farewell, and when they came aboard they commanded the master and the company hastily to get out the ship. The master answered that it was impossible, for that the wind was contrary and overblowed. And he required us, upon forfeiture of our bands, that we should do our endeavour to get her forth. Then went we to warp out the ship, and presently the king sent a boat aboard of us, with three men in her, commanding the said Sonnings to come ashore, at whose coming the king demanded of him custom for the oils. Sonnings answered him that his highness had promised to deliver them customs free. But, notwithstanding, the king weighed not his said promise, and as an infidel that hath not the fear of God before his eyes, nor regard of his word, albeit he was a king, he caused the said Sonnings to pay the custom to the uttermost penny; and afterwards ordered him to make haste away, saying that the janisaries would have the oil ashore again.

These janisaries are soldiers there under the Great Turk, and their power is above the king's. And so the said factor departed from the king, and came to the waterside, and called for a boat to come aboard, and he brought with him the foresaid Patrone Norado. The company, inquisitive to know what man that was, Sonnings answered that he was his countryman, a passenger. "I pray God," said the company, "that we come not into trouble by this man." Then said Sonnings angrily, "What have you to do with any matters of mine? If anything chance otherwise than well, I must answer for all."

Now the Turk unto whom this Patrone Norado was indebted, missing him, supposed him to be aboard of our ship, presently went unto the king and told him that he thought that his pledge, Patrone Norado, was aboard on the English ship. Whereupon the king presently sent a boat aboard of us, with three men in her, commanding the said Sonnings to come ashore; and, not speaking anything as touching the man, he said that he would come presently in his own boat; but as soon as they were gone he willed us to warp forth the ship, and said that he would see the knaves hanged before he would go ashore. And when the king saw that he came not ashore, but still continued warping away the ship, he straight commanded the gunner of the bulwark next unto us to shoot three shots without ball. Then we came all to the said Sonnings, and asked him what the matter was that we were shot at; he said that it was the janisaries who would have the oil ashore again, and willed us to make haste away. And after that he had discharged three shots without ball he commanded all the gunners in the town to do their endeavour to sink us; but the Turkish gunners could not once strike us, wherefore the king sent presently to the Banio (this Banio is the prison whereas all the captives lay at night), and promised that if there were any that could either sink us or else cause us to come in again, he should have a hundred crowns and his liberty. With that came forth a Spaniard called Sebastian, which had been an old servitor in Flanders, and he said that, upon the performance of that promise, he would undertake either to sink us or to cause us to come in again, and thereto he would gage his life; and at the first shot he split our rudder's head in pieces, and the second shot he struck us under water, and the third shot he shot us through our foremast with a culverin shot, and thus, he having rent both our rudder and mast and shot us under water, we were enforced to go in again.

This Sebastian for all his diligence herein had neither his liberty nor a hundred crowns, so promised by the said king; but, after his service done, was committed again to prison, whereby may appear the regard that a Turk or infidel hath of his work, although he be able to perform it—yea, more, though he be a king.

Then our merchants, seeing no remedy, they, together with five of our company, went ashore; and they then ceased shooting. They shot unto us in the whole nine-and-thirty shots without the hurt of any man.

And when our merchants came ashore the king commanded presently that they, with the rest of our company that were with them, should be chained four and four to a hundredweight of iron, and when we came in with the ship there came presently above a hundred Turks aboard of us, and they searched us and stripped our very clothes from our backs, and broke open our chests, and made a spoil of all that we had; and the Christian caitiffs likewise that came aboard of us made spoil of our goods, and used us as ill as the Turks did. And our master's mate, having a Geneva Bible in his hand, there came the king's chief gunner and took it out from him, who showed me of it; and I, having the language, went presently to the king's treasurer, and told him of it, saying that since it was the will of God that we should fall into their hands, yet that they should grant us to use our consciences to our own discretion, as they suffered the Spaniards and other nations to use theirs; and he granted us. Then I told him that the master gunner had taken away a Bible from one of our men: the treasurer went presently and commanded him to deliver up the Bible again, which he did. And within a little after he took it from the man again, and I showed the treasurer of it, and presently he commanded him to deliver it again, saying, "Thou villain! wilt thou turn to Christianity again?" for he was a relagado, which is one that was first a Christian and afterwards becometh a Turk; and so he delivered me the Bible the second time. And then I, having it in my hand, the gunner came to me, and spake these words, saying, "Thou dog! I will have the book in despite of thee!" and took it from me, saying, "If you tell the king's treasurer of it any more, by Mahomet I will be revenged of thee!" Notwithstanding I went the third time unto the king's treasurer, and told him of it; and he came with me, saying thus unto the gunner: "By the head of the Great Turk if thou take it from him again thou shalt have a hundred bastinadoes." And forthwith he delivered me the book, saying he had not the value of a pin of the spoil of the ship—which was the better for him, as hereafter you shall hear; for there was none, either Christian or Turk, that took the value of a pennyworth of our goods from us but perished both body and goods within seventeen months following, as hereafter shall plainly appear.

Then came the guardian Basha, who is the keeper of the king's captives, to fetch us all ashore; and then I, remembering the miserable estate of poor distressed captives in the time of their bondage to those infidels, went to mine own chest, and took out thereof a jar of oil, and filled a basket full of white ruske, to carry ashore with me. But before I came to the Banio the Turkish boys had taken away almost all my bread, and the keeper said, "Deliver me the jar of oil, and when thou comest to the Banio thou shalt have it again;" but I never had it of him any more.

But when I came to the Banio and saw our merchants and all the rest of our company in chains, and we all ready to receive the same reward, what heart is there so hard but would have pitied our cause, hearing or seeing the lamentable greeting there was betwixt us. All this happened the first of May, 1584.

And the second day of the same month the king with all his council sat in judgment upon us. The first that were had forth to be arraigned were the factors and the masters, and the king asked them wherefore they came not ashore when he sent for them. And Romaine Sonnings answered that, though he were a king on shore, and might command there, so was he as touching those that were under him; and therefore said, if any offence be, the fault is wholly in myself and in no other. Then forthwith the king gave judgment that the said Romaine Sonnings should be hanged over the north-east bulwark, from whence he conveyed the forenamed Patrone Norado. And then he called for our master, Andrew Dier, and used few words to him, and so condemned him to be hanged over the walls of the westernmost bulwarks.

Then fell our other factor, named Richard Skegs, upon his knees before the king, and said, "I beseech your highness either to pardon our master or else suffer me to die for him, for he is ignorant of this cause." And then the people of that country, favouring the said Richard Skegs, besought the king to pardon them both. So then the king spake these words: "Behold, for thy sake I pardon the master." Then presently the Turks shouted and cried, saying, "Away with the master from the presence of the king." And then he came into the Banio where we were, and told us what had happened, and we all rejoiced at the good hap of Master Skegs, that he was saved, and our master for his sake.

But afterwards our joy was turned to double sorrow, for in the meantime the king's mind was altered: for that one of his council had advised him that, unless the master died also, by the law they could not confiscate the ship nor goods, neither make captive any of the men. Whereupon the king sent for our master again, and gave him another judgment after his pardon for one cause, which was that he should be hanged. Here all true Christians may see what trust a Christian man may put in an infidel's promise, who, being a king, pardoned a man now, as you have heard, and within an hour after hanged him for the same cause before a whole multitude; and also promised our factors their oils custom free, and at their going away made them pay the uttermost penny for the custom thereof.

And when that Romaine Sonnings saw no remedy but that he should die, he protested to turn Turk, hoping thereby to have saved his life. Then said the Turk, "If thou wilt turn Turk, speak the words that thereunto belong;" and he did so. Then said they unto him, "Now thou shalt die in the faith of a Turk;" and so he did, as the Turks reported that were at his execution; and the forenamed Patrone Norado, whereas before he had liberty and did nothing, he then was condemned slave perpetual, except there were payment made of the foresaid sum of money.

Then the king condemned all us, who were in number five and twenty, of which two were hanged (as you have heard) and one died the first day we came on shore by the visitation of Almighty God, and the other three and twenty he condemned slaves perpetually unto the Great Turk, and the ship and goods were confiscated to the use of the Great Turk; then we all fell down upon our knees, giving God thanks for this sorrowful visitation and giving ourselves wholly to the almighty power of God, unto whom all secrets are known, that He of His goodness would vouchsafe to look upon us.

Here may all true Christian hearts see the wonderful works of God showed upon such infidels, blasphemers, and runagate Christians, and so you shall read in the end of this book of the like upon the unfaithful king and all his children, and of as many as took any portion of the said goods.

But first to show our miserable bondage and slavery, and unto what small pittance and allowance we were tied, for every five men had allowance but five aspers of bread in a day, which is but twopence English, and our lodging was to lie on the bare boards, with a very simple cape to cover us. We were also forcibly and most violently shaven, head and beard, and within three days after, I and five more of my fellows, together with fourscore Italians and Spaniards, were sent forth in a galiot to take a Greek carmosel, which came into Arabia to steal negroes, and went out of Tripolis unto that place which was two hundred and forty leagues thence; but we were chained three and three to an oar, and we rowed naked above the girdle, and the boatswain of the galley walked abaft the mast, and his mate afore the mast, and each of them a whip in their hands, and when their devilish choler rose they would strike the Christians for no cause, and they allowed us but half a pound of bread a man in a day, without any other kind of sustenance, water excepted. And when we came to the place where we saw the carmosel, we were not suffered to have neither needle, bodkin, knife, or any other instrument about us, nor at any other time in the night, upon pain of one hundred bastinadoes: we were then also cruelly manacled, in such sort that we could not put our hands the length of one foot asunder the one from the other, and every night they searched our chains three times, to see if they were fast riveted. We continued the fight with the carmosel three hours, and then we took it, and lost but two of our men in that fight; but there were slain of the Greeks five, and fourteen were cruelly hurt; and they that were found were presently made slaves, and chained to the oars, and within fifteen days after we returned again into Tripolis, and then we were put to all manner of slavery. I was put to hew stones, and other to carry stones, and some to draw the cart with earth, and some to make mortar, and some to draw stones (for at that time the Turks builded a church), and thus we were put to all kinds of slavery that was to be done. And in the time of our being there the Moors, that are the husbandmen of the country, rebelled against the king, because he would have constrained them to pay greater tribute than heretofore they had done, so that the soldiers of Tripolis marched forth of the town, to have joined battle against the Moors for their rebellion, and the king sent with them four pieces of ordnance, which were drawn by the captives twenty miles into the country after them, and at the sight thereof the Moors fled, and then the captains returned back again. Then I, and certain Christians more, were sent twelve miles into the country with a cart to load timber, and we returned again the same day.

Now, the king had eighteen captives, which three times a week went to fetch wood thirty miles from the town, and on a time he appointed me for one of the eighteen, and we departed at eight of the clock in the night; and upon the way, as we rode upon the camels, I demanded of one of our company who did direct us the way: he said that there was a Moor in our company which was our guide; and I demanded of them how Tripolis and the wood bare one off the other, and he said, "East-north-east and west-south-west." And at midnight, or thereabouts, as I was riding upon my camel, I fell asleep, and the guide and all the rest rode away from me, not thinking but I had been among them. When I awoke, and finding myself alone, I durst not call nor holloa, for fear lest the wild Moors should hear me—because they hold this opinion, that in killing a Christian they do God good service—and musing with myself what were best for me to do: if I should return back to Tripolis without any wood or company I should be most miserably used; therefore, of the two evils, rather I had to go forth to the losing of my life than to turn back and trust to their mercy, fearing to be used as before I had seen others. For, understanding by some of my company before how Tripolis and the said wood did lie one off another, by the North Star I went forth at adventure, and, as God would have it, I came right to the place where they were, even about an hour before day. There altogether we rested, and gave our camels provender, and as soon as the day appeared we rode all into the wood; and I, seeing no wood there but a stick here and a stick there, about the bigness of a man's arm, growing in the sand, it caused me to marvel how so many camels should be loaded in that place. The wood was juniper; we needed no axe nor edged tool to cut it, but plucked it up by strength of hands, roots and all, which a man might easily do, and so gathered together a little at one place, and so at another, and laded our camels, and came home about seven of the clock that night following: because I fell lame and my camel was tired, I left my wood in the way.

There was in Tripolis at that time a Venetian whose name was Benedetto Venetiano, and seventeen captives more of his countrymen, which ran away from Tripolis in a boat and came inside of an island called Malta, which lieth forty leagues from Tripolis right north; and, being within a mile of the shore and very fair weather, one of their company said, *In dispetto de Dio adesso venio a pilliar terra,* which is as much to say: "In the despite of God, I shall now fetch the shore;" and presently there arose a mighty storm, with thunder and rain, and the wind at the north, their boat being very small, so that they were enforced to bear up room and to sheer right afore the wind over against the coast of Barbary, from whence they came, and rowing up and down the coast, their victuals being spent, the twenty-first day after their departure, they were enforced through the want of food to come ashore, thinking to have stolen some sheep. But the Moors of the country very craftily (perceiving their intent) gathered together a threescore of horsemen and hid themselves behind the sandy hill, and when the Christians were come all ashore, and passed by half a mile into the country, the Moors rode betwixt them and their boat, and some of them pursued the Christians, and so they were all taken and brought to Tripolis, from whence they had before escaped; and presently the king commanded that the foresaid Benedetto, with one more of his company, should lose their ears, and the rest to be most cruelly beaten, which was presently done. This king had a son which was a ruler in an island called Gerbi, whereunto arrived an English ship called the *Green Dragon*, of the which was master one M. Blonket, who, having a very unhappy boy on that ship, and understanding that whosoever would turn Turk should be well entertained of the king's son, this boy did run ashore and voluntarily turned Turk. Shortly after the king's son came to Tripolis to visit his father, and seeing our company, he greatly fancied Richard Burges, our purser, and James Smith. They were both young men, therefore he was very desirous to have them to turn Turks; but they would not yield to his desire, saying, "We are your father's slaves and as slaves we will serve him." Then his father the king sent for them, and asked them if they would turn Turks; and they said: "If it please your Highness, Christians we were born and so we will remain, and beseech the king that they might not be enforced thereunto." The king had there before in his house a son of a yeoman of our Queen's guard, whom the king's son had enforced to turn Turk; his name was John Nelson. Him the king caused to be brought to these young men, and then said unto them, "Will you not bear this, your countryman, company, and be Turk as he is?" and they said that they would not yield thereunto during life. But it fell out that, within a month after, the king's son went home to Gerbi again, being five score miles from Tripolis, and carried our two foresaid young men with him, which were Richard Burges and James Smith. And after their departure from us they sent us a letter, signifying that there was no violence showed unto them as yet; yet within three days after they were violently used, for that the king's son demanded of them again if that they would turn Turk. Then answered Richard Burges: "A Christian I am, and so I will remain." Then the king's son very angrily said unto him, "By Mahomet thou shalt presently be made Turk!" Then called he for his men and commanded them to make him Turk; and they did so, and circumcised him, and would have had him speak the words that thereunto belonged; but he answered them stoutly that he would not, and although they had put on him the habit of a Turk, yet said he, "A Christian I was born, and so I will remain, though you force me to do otherwise."

And then he called for the other, and commanded him to be made Turk perforce also; but he was very strong, for it was so much as eight of the king's son's men could do to hold him. So in the end they circumcised him and made him Turk. Now, to pass over a little, and so to show the manner of our deliverance out of that miserable captivity.

In May aforesaid, shortly after our apprehension,

I wrote a letter into England unto my father, dwelling in Evistoke in Devonshire, signifying unto him the whole estate of our calamities, and I wrote also to Constantinople to the English ambassador, both which letters were faithfully delivered. But when my father had received my letter, and understood the truth of our mishap, and the occasion thereof, and what had happened to the offenders, he certified the Right Honourable the Earl of Bedford thereof, who in short space acquainted her Highness with the whole cause thereof; and her Majesty, like a most merciful princess tendering her subjects, presently took order for our deliverance. Whereupon the Right Worshipful Sir Edward Osborne, knight, directed his letters with all speed to the English ambassador in Constantinople to procure our delivery, and he obtained the Great Turk's commission, and sent it forthwith to Tripolis by one Master Edward Barton, together with a justice of the Great Turk's and one soldier, and another Turk and a Greek, which was his interpreter, which could speak beside Greek, Turkish, Italian, Spanish and English. And when they came to Tripolis they were well entertained, and the first night they did lie in a captain's house in the town. All our company that were in Tripolis came that night for joy to

Master Barton and the other commissioners to see them. Then Master Barton said unto us, "Welcome, my good countrymen," and lovingly entertained us; and at our departure from him he gave us two shillings, and said, "Serve God, for to-morrow I hope you shall be as free as ever you were." We all gave him thanks and so departed.

The next day, in the morning very early, the king having intelligence of their coming, sent word to the keeper that none of the Englishmen (meaning our company) should go to work. Then he sent for Master Barton and the other commissioners, and demanded of the said Master Barton his message. The justice answered that the Great Turk, his sovereign, had sent them unto him, signifying that he was informed that a certain English ship, called the *Jesus*, was by him the said king confiscated about twelve months since, and now my said sovereign hath here sent his especial commission by us unto you for the deliverance of the said ship and goods, and also the free liberty and deliverance of the Englishmen of the said ship whom you have taken and kept in captivity. And further, the same justice said, I am authorised by my said sovereign the Great Turk to see it done; and therefore I command you, by the virtue of this commission, presently to make restitution of the premises or the value thereof. And so did the justice deliver unto the king the Great Turk's commission to the effect aforesaid, which commission the king with all obedience received; and after the perusing of the same, he forthwith commanded all the English captives to be brought before him, and then willed the keeper to strike off all our irons. Which done, the king said, "You Englishmen, for that you did offend the laws of this place, by the same laws therefore some of your company were condemned to die, as you know, and you to be perpetual captives during your lives; notwithstanding, seeing it hath pleased my sovereign lord the Great Turk to pardon your said offences, and to give you your freedom and liberty, behold, here I make delivery of you unto this English gentleman." So he delivered us all that were there, being thirteen in number, to Master Barton, who required also those two young men which the king's son had taken with him. Then the king answered that it was against their law to deliver them, for that they were turned Turks; and, touching the ship and goods, the king said that he had sold her, but would make restitution of the value, and as much of the goods as came unto his hands. And so the king arose and went to dinner, and commanded a Jew to go with

Master Barton and the other commissioners to show them their lodgings, which was a house provided and appointed them by the said king. And because I had the Italian and Spanish tongues, by which there most traffic in that country is, Master Barton made me his caterer, to buy his victuals for him and his company, and he delivered me money needful for the same. Thus were we set at liberty the 28th day of April, 1585.

Now, to return to the king's plagues and punishments which Almighty God at his will and pleasure sendeth upon men in the sight of the world, and likewise of the plagues that befell his children and others aforesaid. First, when we were made bondmen, being the second day of May, 1584, the king had 300 captives, and before the month was expired there died of them of the plague 150. And whereas there were twenty-six men of our company, of whom two were hanged and one died the same day as we were made bondslaves, that present month there died nine more of our company of the plague, and other two were forced to turn Turks as before rehearsed; and on the 4th day of June next following, the king lost 150 camels which were taken from him by the wild Moors; and on the 28th day of the said month of June one Geffrey Malteese, a renegado of Malta, ran away to his country, and stowed a brigantine which the king had builded for to take the Christians withal, and carried with him twelve Christians more which were the king's captives. Afterwards about the 10th day of July next following, the king rode forth upon the greatest and fairest mare that might be seen, as white as any swan; he had not ridden forty paces from his house, but on a sudden the same mare fell down under him stark dead, and I with six more were commanded to bury her, skin, shoes, and all, which we did. And about three months after our delivery, Master Barton, with all the residue of his company, departed from Tripolis to Zante in a vessel called a settea, of one Marcus Segoorus, who dwelt in Zante; and, after our arrival at Zante, we remained fifteen days there aboard our vessel, before we could have *Platego* (that is, leave to come ashore), because the plague was in that place from whence we came, and about three days after we came ashore, thither came another settea of Marseilles, bound for Constantinople. Then did Master Barton and his company, with two more of our company, ship themselves as passengers in the same settea and went to Constantinople. But the other nine of us that remained in Zante, about three months after, shipped ourselves in a ship of the said Marcus Segoorus, which came to Zante, and was bound for England. In which three months the soldiers of Tripolis killed the said king; and then the king's son, according to the custom there, went to Constantinople, to surrender up all his father's treasure, goods, captives, and concubines unto the Great Turk, and took with him our said purser Richard Burges, and James Smith, and also the other two Englishmen which he the king's son had enforced to become Turks as is aforesaid. And they, the said Englishmen, finding now some opportunity, concluded with the Christian captives which were going with them unto Constantinople, being in number about 150, to kill the king's son and all the Turks which were aboard of the galley, and privily the said Englishmen conveyed unto the said Christian captives weapons for that purpose. And when they came into the main sea, towards Constantinople (upon the faithful promise of the said Christian captives) these four Englishmen leapt suddenly into the crossia— that is, into the middest of the galley, where the cannon lieth—and with their swords drawn, did fight against all the foresaid Turks, and for want of help of the said Christian captives, who falsely brake their promises, the said Master Blonket's boy was killed and the said James Smith, and our purser Richard Burges, and the other Englishmen were taken and bound into chains, to be hanged at their arrival in Constantinople. And, as the Lord's will was, about two days after, passing through the Gulf of Venice, at an island called Cephalonia, they met with two of the Duke of Venice, his galleys, which took that galley, and killed the king's son and his mother, and all the Turks that were there, in number 150, and they saved the Christian captives; and would have killed the two Englishmen, because they were circumcised and become Turks, had not the other Christian captives excused them, saying that they were enforced to be Turks by the king's son, and showed the Venetians how they did enterprise at sea to fight against all the Turks, and that their two fellows were slain in that fight. Then the Venetians saved them, and they, with all the residue of the said captives, had their liberty, which were in number 150 or thereabouts, and the said galley and all the Turks' treasure was confiscated to the use of the State of Venice. And from thence our two Englishmen travelled homeward by land, and in this meantime we had one more of our company which died in Zante, and afterwards the other eight shipped themselves at Zante in a ship of the said Marcus Segoorus which was bound for England. And before we departed thence, there arrived the *Ascension* and the *George Bonaventure* of London, in Cephalonia, in a harbour there called Arrogostoria, whose merchants agreed with the merchants of our ship, and so laded all the merchandise of our ship into the said ships of London, who took us eight also in as passengers, and so we came home. And within two months after our arrival at London our said purser Richard Burges, and his fellow, came home also, for the which we are bound to praise Almighty God during our lives, and, as duty bindeth us, to pray for the preservation of our most gracious Queen, for the great care her Majesty had over us, her poor subjects, in seeking and procuring of our deliverance aforesaid, and also for her Honourable Privy Council; and I especially for the prosperity and good estate of the house of the late deceased, the Right Honourable the Earl of Bedford, whose honour I must confess most diligently, at the suit of my father now departed, travailed herein—for the which I rest continually bounden to him, whose soul I doubt not but already is in the heavens in joy, with the Almighty, unto which place He vouchsafed to bring us all, that for our sins suffered most vile and shameful death upon the cross, there to live perpetually world without end. Amen.

The Queen's letters to the Turk, 1584, *for the restitution of the ship, called the* Jesus, *and the English captives detained in Tripolis, in Barbary, and for certain other prisoners in Algiers.*

Elizabeth, by the grace of the Most High God and only Maker of Heaven and Earth, of England, France, and Ireland Queen, and of the Christian faith, against all the idolaters and false professors of the name of Christ dwelling among the Christians, most invincible and puissant Defender; to the most valiant and invincible Prince, Sultan Murad Can, the most mighty ruler of the Kingdom of Mussulman and of the East Empire, the only and highest monarch above all, health and many happy and fortunate years, with great abundance of the best things.

Most noble and puissant Emperor, about two years now past, we wrote unto your Imperial Majesty that our well-beloved servant, William Harebrown, a man of great reputation and honour, might be received under your high authority for our ambassador in Constantinople and other places, under the obedience of your Empire of Mussulman; and also that the Englishmen being our subjects might exercise intercourse and merchandise in all those provinces no less freely than the French, Polonians, Venetians, Germans, and other your confederates, which travel through divers of the East parts: endeavouring that by mutual traffic the East may be joined and knit to the West.

Which privileges, when as your most puissant Majesty by your letters and under your dispensation most liberally and favourably granted to our subjects of England, we could no less do but in thát respect give you as great thanks as our heart could conceive, trusting that it will come to pass that this order of traffic so well ordained will bring with itself most great profits and commodities to both sides, as well to the parties subject to your Empire as to the provinces of our Kingdom.

. Which thing, that it may be done in plain and effectual manner, whereas some of our subjects of late at Tripolis in Barbary, and at Algiers, were by the inhabitants of those places (being perhaps ignorant of your pleasure) evil intreated and grievously vexed, we do friendly and lovingly desire your Imperial Majesty that you will understand their causes by our ambassador, and afterward give commandment to the lieutenants and presidents of those provinces, that our people may henceforth freely, without any violence or injury, travel and do their business in those places.

And we again with all endeavour shall study to perform all those things which we shall in any wise understand to be acceptable to your Imperial Majesty, which God, the only Maker of the World, Most Best and Most Great, long keep in health and flourishing. Given in our Palace at London, the 5th day of the month of September, in the year of Jesus Christ our Saviour 1584, and of our reign the twenty-sixth.

The commandment obtained of the Grand Signior by her Majesty's ambassador, for the quiet passing of her subjects to and from his dominions, sent in Anno 1584 to the Viceroys, Algiers, Tunis, and Tripolis in Barbary.

To our Beglerbeg of Algiers. We certify thee by this our commandment that the right honourable William Harebrowne, ambassador to the Queen's Majesty of England, hath signified unto us that the ships of that country, in their coming and returning to and from our Empire, on the one part of the seas have the Spaniards, Florentines, Sicilians, and Maltese, on the other part our countries, committed to your charge, which above said Christians will not quietly suffer their egress and regress into and out of our dominions, but to take and make the men captives, and forfeit the ships and goods, as the last year the Maltese did one which they took at Gerbi, and to that end do continually lie in wait for them to their destruction, whereupon they are constrained to stand to their defence at any such times as they might meet with them; wherefore considering by this means they must stand upon their guard when they shall see any galley afar off, whereby if meeting with any of your galleys, and not knowing them, in their defence they do shoot at them, and yet after, when they do certainly know them, do not shoot any more, but require to pass peaceably on their voyage, which you would deny, saying, "The peace is broken, for that you have shot at us, and so do make prize of them, contrary to our privileges, and against reason:" for the preventing of which inconvenience the said ambassador hath required this our commandment. We therefore command thee that upon sight hereof thou do not permit any such matter in no sort whatsoever, but suffer the said Englishmen to pass in peace, according to the tenor of our commandment given, without any disturbance or let by any means upon the way, although that, meeting with thy galleys, and not knowing them afar off, they, taking them for enemies, should shoot at them, yet shall ye not suffer them to hurt them therefor, but quietly to pass. Wherefore look thou, that they may have right according to our privilege given them, and finding any that absenteth himself and will not obey this our commandment, presently certify us to our porch, that we may give order for his punishment; and with reverence give faithful credit to this our commandment, which having read, thou shalt again return it unto them that present it. From our palace in Constantinople, the prime of June, 1584.

The Turk's letter to the King of Tripolis, in Barbary, commanding the restitution of an English ship, called the Jesus, *with the men and goods, sent from Constantinople by Mahomet Beg, a justice of the Great Turk's, and an English gentleman, called Master Edward Barton. Anno* 1584.

Honourable and most worthy Pasha Romadan Beglerbeg, most wise and prudent judge of the West Tripolis, we wish the end of all thy enterprises happy and prosperous. By these our Highness's letters we certify thee that the Right Honourable William Harebrowne, Ambassador in our most famous porch for the most excellent Queen's Majesty of England, in person and by letters hath certified our Highness that a certain ship, with all her furniture and artillery, worth two thousand ducats, arriving in the port of Tripolis, and discharged of her lading and merchandise, paid our custom according to order, and again the merchants laded their ship with oil, which by constraint they were enforced to buy of you, and having answered in like manner the custom for the same, determined to depart. A Frenchman, assistant to the merchant, unknown to the Englishmen, carried away with him another Frenchman indebted to a certain Moor in four hundred ducats, and by force caused the Englishmen and ship to depart, who, neither suspecting fraud nor deceit, hoisted sails. In the meantime, this man, whose debtor the Frenchman had stolen away, went to the Pasha with a supplication, by whose means, and force of the Castle, the Englishmen were constrained to return into the port, where the Frenchman, author of the evil, with the master of the ship, an Englishman, innocent of the crime, were hanged, and five-and-twenty Englishmen cast into prison, of whom, through famine and thirst, and stink of the prison, eleven died, and the rest were like to die. Further, it was signified to our Majesty also that the merchandise and other goods with the ship were worth seven thousand six hundred ducats. Which things, if they be so, this is our commandment, which was granted and given by our Majesty, that the English ship, and all the merchandise, and whatsoever else was taken away, be wholly restored, and that the Englishmen be let go free, and suffered to return into their country. Wherefore, when this our commandment shall come unto thee, we straightly command that the foresaid business be diligently looked unto and discharged. And if it be so that a Frenchman, and no Englishman, hath done this craft and wickedness, unknown to the Englishmen, and, as author of the wickedness, is punished, and that the Englishmen committed nothing against the peace and league, or their articles; also, if they paid custom according to order, it is against law, custom of countries, and their privilege, to hinder or hurt them. Neither is it meet their ship, merchandise, and all their goods taken should be withholden. We will, therefore, that the English ship, merchandise, and all other their goods, without exception, be restored to the Englishmen; also, that the men be let go free, and, if they will, let none hinder them to return peaceably into their country; do not commit that they another time complain of this matter, and how this business is despatched certify us at our most famous porch. Dated in the city of Constantinople, in the nine hundred and ninety-second year of Mahomet, and in the end of the month of October, and the year of Jesus 1584.

A letter of Master William Harebrowne, the English Ambassador, Ledger in Constantinople, to the Pasha Romadan, the Beglerbeg of Tripolis, in Barbary, for the restoring of an English ship, called the Jesus, *with goods and men detained as slaves*, 1585.

Right Honourable Lord, it hath been signified unto us by divers letters, what hath fallen out concerning a certain ship of ours, called the *Jesus*, into which, for the help of Richard Skegs, one of our merchants in the same, now deceased, there was admitted a certain Frenchman, called Romaine Sonnings, which for his ill behaviour, according to his deserts, seeking to carry away with him another Frenchman, which was indebted to certain of your people, without paying his creditors, was hanged by sentence of justice, together with Andrew Dier, the master of the said ship, who, simply and without fraud, giving credit to the said Frenchman, without any knowledge of this evil fact, did not return when he was commanded by your honourable lordship. The death of the said lewd Frenchman we approve as a thing well done, but contrariwise, whereas your lordship hath confiscated the said ship, with the goods therein, and hath made slaves of the mariners, as a thing altogether contrary to the privileges of the Grand Signior, granted four years since, and confirmed by us, on the behalf of the most excellent the Queen's Majesty of England, our mistress, and altogether contrary to the league of the said Grand Signior, who, being fully informed of the aforesaid cause, hath granted unto us his royal commandment of restitution, which we send unto your honourable lordship by the present bearer, Edward Barton, our secretary, and Mahomet Beg, one of the justices of his stately court, with other letters of the most excellent Admiral and most valiant captain of the sea, requiring your most honourable lordship, as well on the behalf of the Grand Signior as of the Queen's most Excellent Majesty, my mistress, that the men, oils, ship, furniture, money, and all other goods whatsoever, by your lordship and your order taken from our men, be restored unto this my secretary freely, without delay, as the Grand Signior of his goodness hath granted unto us, especially in regard that the same oils were bought by the commandment of our Queen's most Excellent Majesty for the provision of her Court. Which if you perform not, we protest by these our letters against you, that you are the cause of all the inconveniences which may ensue upon this occasion, as the author thereof contrary to the holy league sworn by both our princes, as by the privileges, which this our servant will show you, may appear. For the seeing of which league performed, we remain here as Ledger in this stately court, and by this means you shall answer in another world unto God alone, and in this world unto the Grand Signior, for this heinous sin committed by you against so many poor souls, which by this your cruelty are in part dead, and in part detained by you in most miserable captivity. Contrariwise, if it shall please you to avoid this mischief, and to remain in the favour of Almighty God and of our princes, you shall friendly fulfil this our just demand (as it behoveth you to show yourself a prudent governor and faithful servant unto your lord), and the same may turn to your great honour and profit by the trade of merchandise, which our men in time to come may use in that government of yours, which, generally, as well those poor men as all others which you shall meet at the sea, ought to be, according to the commandment of the Grand Signior, friendly entertained and received of your honourable lordship; and we will not fail in the duties of a special friend whensoever you shall have occasion to use us as we desire. Almighty God grant unto your lordship (in the fulfilling of this our just request, whereby we may be delivered from further trouble in this matter and yourself from further displeasure) all true felicity and increase of honour. Given in our palace from Capamat, in Pera, the 15th of January, 1585.

A brief extract specifying the certain daily payments, answered quarterly in time of peace, by the Grand Signior, out of his treasury, to the officers of his Seraglio or Court, successively in degrees; collected in a yearly total sum as followeth:

For his own diet every day, one thousand and one aspers, according to a former custom received from his ancestors; notwithstanding that otherwise his diurnal expense is very much, and not certainly known, which sum maketh sterling money by the year, two thousand one hundred and ninety-two pounds, three shillings, and eightpence.

The forty-five thousand janisaries, reparted into sundry places of his dominions, at five aspers a day, amounteth by the year, five hundred fourscore and eleven thousand and three hundred pounds.

The azamoglans' tribute children far surmount

that number, for that they are collected from among the Christians, from whom between the years of five and twelve they are pulled away yearly perforce; whereof I suppose those in service may be equal in number with the janisaries abovesaid, at three aspers a day, one with another, which is two hundred fourscore and fifteen thousand five hundred and fifty pounds.

The five Pashas whereof the Viceroy is supreme, at one thousand aspers the day, besides their yearly revenues, amounteth sterling by the year, ten thousand nine hundred and fifty pounds.

The five Beglerbegs, chief presidents of Greece, Hungary, and Slavonia, being in Europe, in Anatolia, and Carmania of Asia, at one thousand aspers the day; as also to eighteen other governors of provinces at five hundred aspers the day, amounteth by the year thirty thousand five hundred and threescore pounds.

The Pasha, admiral of the sea, one thousand aspers the day, two thousand one hundred fourscore and ten thousand pounds.

The Aga of the janisaries, general of the footmen, five hundred aspers the day, and maketh by the year in sterling money one thousand fourscore and fifteen pounds.

The Imbrahur Pasha, master of his horse, one

hundred and fifty aspers the day, in sterling money three hundred and eight and twenty pounds.

The chief esquire under him, one hundred and fifty aspers, is three hundred and eight and twenty pounds.

The Agas of the Spahi, captains of the horsemen, five at one hundred and fifty aspers to either of them, maketh sterling one thousand nine hundred threescore and eleven pounds.

The Capagi Pashas, head porters, four, one hundred and fifty aspers to each, and maketh out in sterling money by the year, one thousand three hundred and fourteen pounds.

The Sisinghir Pasha, controller of the household, one hundred and twenty aspers the day, and maketh out in sterling money by the year, two hundred threescore and two pounds, sixteen shillings.

The Chiaus Pasha, captain of the pensioners, one hundred and twenty aspers the day, and amounteth to, by the year, in sterling money, two hundred threescore and two pounds, sixteen shillings.

The Capigilar Caiafi, captain of his barge, one hundred and twenty aspers the day, and maketh out by the year, in sterling money, two hundred threescore and two pounds, sixteen shillings.

The Solach Bassi, captain of his guard, one hundred and twenty aspers, two hundred threescore and two pounds, sixteen shillings.

The Giebrigi Bassi, master of the armoury, one hundred and twenty aspers, two hundred threescore and two pounds, sixteen shillings.

The Topagi Bassi, master of the artillery, one hundred and twenty aspers, two hundred threescore and two pounds, sixteen shillings.

The Echim Bassi, physician to his person, one hundred and twenty aspers, two hundred threescore and two pounds, sixteen shillings.

The forty physicians under him, to each forty aspers is three thousand eight hundred threescore and six pounds, sixteen shillings.

The Mustafaracas, spearmen attending on his person, in number 500, to either threescore aspers, and maketh sterling threescore and five thousand and seven hundred pounds.

The Cisingeri, gentlemen attending upon his diet, forty, at forty aspers each of them, and amounteth to sterling by the year, three thousand five hundred and four pounds.

The Chiausi, pensioners, four hundred and forty, at thirty aspers, twenty-eight thousand nine hundred and eight pounds.

The Capagi, porters of the Court and city, four

hundred at eight aspers, and maketh sterling money by the year, seven thousand and eight pounds.

The Solachi, archers of his guard, three hundred and twenty, at nine aspers, and cometh unto, in English money, the sum of six thousand three hundred and six pounds.

The Spahi, men of arms of the Court and the city, ten thousand, at twenty-five aspers, and maketh of English money, five hundred forty and seven thousand and five hundred pounds.

The Janisaries, sixteen thousand, at six aspers, is two hundred and ten thousand and two hundred and forty pounds.

The Giebegi, furbishers of armour, one thousand five hundred, at six aspers, and amounteth to sterling money, nineteen thousand seven hundred and fourscore pounds.

The Seiefir, servitors in his esquire or stable, five hundred, at two aspers, and maketh sterling money, two thousand one hundred fourscore and ten pounds.

The Saefi, saddlers and bit-makers, five hundred, at seven aspers, seven thousand six hundred threescore and five pounds.

The Capergi, carriers upon mules, two hundred, at five aspers, two thousand one hundred fourscore and ten pounds.

The Ginegi, carriers upon camels, one thousand five hundred, at eight aspers, and amounteth in sterling money to twenty-six thousand two hundred and fourscore pounds.

The Reiz, or captains of the galleys, three hundred, at ten aspers, and amounteth in English money, by the year, the sum of six thousand five hundred threescore and ten pounds.

The Alechingi, masters of the said galleys, three hundred, at seven aspers, four thousand five hundred fourscore and nineteen pounds.

The Getti, boatswains thereof, three hundred, at six aspers, is three thousand nine hundred forty and two pounds.

The Oda Bassi, pursers, three hundred, at five aspers, maketh three thousand two hundred and fourscore pounds.

The Azappi, soldiers, two thousand six hundred, at four aspers, whereof the five hundred do continually keep the galleys, two-and-twenty thousand seven hundred fourscore and six pounds.

The Mariers Bassi, masters over the shipwrights and caulkers of the navy, nine, at twenty aspers the piece, amounteth to three thousand fourscore and four pounds, four shillings.

The Master Dassi, shipwrights and caulkers, one thousand, at fourteen aspers, and amounteth to, by the year, thirty thousand six hundred and threescore pounds.

Summa totalis of daily payments amounteth by the year sterling one million nine hundred threescore eight thousand seven hundred and thirty-five pounds, nineteen shillings, and eight pence, answered quarterly without default with the sum of four hundred fourscore twelve thousand one hundred fourscore and four pounds, four shillings, and eleven pence, and is for every day five thousand three hundred fourscore and thirteen pounds, fifteen shillings, and ten pence.

Annuities of lands never improved five times more in value than their sums mentioned, given by the said Grand Signior as followeth:

To the Viceroy for his timar or annuity, 60,000 gold ducats.

To the second pasha for his annuity, 50,000 ducats.

To the third pasha for his annuity, 40,000 ducats.

To the fourth pasha for his annuity, 30,000 ducats.

To the fifth pasha for his annuity, 20,000 ducats.

To the captain of the janisaries, 20,000 ducats.

To the Jou Merhor Bassi, master of his horse, 15,000 ducats.

To the captain of the pensioners, 10,000 ducats.

To the captain of his guard, 5,000 ducats.

Summa totalis, 90,000 livres sterling.

Besides these above specified be sundry other annuities, given to divers others of his aforesaid officers, as also to certain persons called Sahims, diminishing from three thousand to two hundred ducats, esteemed treble to surmount the annuity abovesaid.

The Turk's Chief Officers.

The Viceroy is high treasurer, notwithstanding that under him be three sub-treasurers, called Testaders, which be accountable to him of the receipts out of Europe, Asia, and Africa, save their yearly annuity of lands.

The Lord Chancellor is called Nissangi Pasha, who sealeth with a certain proper character such licenses, safe-conducts, passports, especial grants, etc., as proceed from the Grand Signior; notwithstanding all letters to foreign princes so firmed be after enclosed in a bag and sealed by the Grand Signior, with a signet which he ordinarily weareth about his neck, credited of them to have been of ancient appertaining to King Solomon the Wise.

The Admiral giveth his voice in the election of all begies, captains of islands (to whom he giveth their charge), as also appointeth the sub-pashas, bailies or constables over cities and towns upon the sea-coasts about Constantinople and in the Archipelago, whereof he reapeth great profit.

The Sub-bassi of Pera payeth him nearly fifteen thousand ducats, and so likewise either of the others, according as they are placed.

The Resistop serveth in office to the Viceroy and Chancellor as secretary, and so likewise doth the Cogy, Master of the Rolls, before which two pass all writings presented to or granted by the said Viceroy and Chancellor, offices of especial credit and like profit, moreover rewarded with annuities of lands.

There be also two chief judges named Ladies Lisguire, the one over Europe and the other over Asia and Africa, which in court do sit on the bench at the left hand of the pashas. These sell all offices to the under-judges of the land called Cadies, whereof is one in every city or town, before whom all matters of controversy are by judgment decided, as also penalties and corrections for crimes ordained to be executed upon the offenders by the Sub-bassi.

The number of Soldiers continually attending upon the Beglerbegs, the Governors of Provinces, and Sangiacks, and their petty Captains maintained of these Provinces.

The Beglerbegs of
{
Græcia	40,000
Buda	15,000
Slavonia	15,000
Anatolia	15,000
Caramania	15,000
Armenia	18,000
Persia	20,000
Usdrum	15,000
Chirusta	15,000
Caræmiti	30,000
Giersul	32,000
Bagdad	25,000
Balsara	22,000
Lassaija	17,000
Aleppo	25,000
Damascus	17,000
Cairo	12,000
Abes	12,000
Mecca	8,000
Cyprus	18,000
Tunis, in Barbary	8,000
Tripolis, in Syria	8,000
Algiers	40,000
} Persons.

Whose sangiacks and petty captains be three hundred and sixty-eight, every of which retaining continually in pay from five hundred to two hundred soldiers, may be, one with another, at least three hundred thousand persons.

Chief Officers in his Seraglio about his person be these:

Capiaga, high porter.
Alnader Bassi, treasurer.
Oda Bassi, chamberlain.
Killergi Bassi, steward.
Saraiaga, controller.
Peskerolen, groom of the chamber.
Edostoglan, gentleman of the ewer.
Sehetaraga, armour-bearer.
Choataraga, he that carrieth his riding cloak.
Ebietaraga, groom of the stool.

There be many other meaner offices, which I esteem superfluous to write.

The Turk's Yearly Revenue.

The Grand Signior's annual revenue is said to be fourteen millions and a half of golden ducats, which is sterling five millions eightscore thousand pounds.

The tribute paid by the Christians, his subjects,

is one gold ducat yearly for the redemption of every head, which may amount unto not so little as one million of golden ducats, which is sterling three hundred and threescore thousand pounds.

Moreover, in time of war he exacteth manifold sums, for maintenance of his army and navy, of the said Christians.

. The Emperor payeth him yearly tribute for Hungary threescore thousand dollars, which is sterling thirteen thousand pounds, besides presents to the Viceroy and pashas, which are said to surmount twenty thousand dollars.

Ambassadors' Allowances.

The ambassador of the Emperor is allowed one thousand aspers the day.

The ambassador of the French king heretofore enjoyed the like; but of late years, by means of displeasure conceived by Mahomet, then Viceroy, it was reduced to six crowns the day, besides the provision of his esquire of stable.

The ambassador of Poland and for the State of Venice are not Ledgers as these two abovesaid. The said Polack is allowed twelve French crowns the day during his abode, which may be for a month. Very seldom do the State of Venice send any ambassador otherwise than enforced of urgent necessity; but instead thereof keep there their agent, president over their merchants, of them termed a bailiff, who hath no allowance of the Grand Signior, although his port and state is in manner as magnifical as the other aforesaid ambassadors'. The Spanish ambassador was equal with others in janisaries; but for so much as he would not, according to custom, follow the list of other ambassadors in making presents to the Grand Signior, he had no allowance. His abode there was three years, at the end whereof, having concluded a truce for six years, taking place from his first coming in November last past, he was never admitted to the presence of the Grand Signior.

A TRUE REPORT OF A WORTHY FIGHT,

Performed in the voyage from Turkey by five ships of London, against eleven galleys and two frigates of the King of Spain's, at Pantalarea, within the Straits, Anno 1586. Written by PHILIP JONES.

THE merchants of London, being of the incorporation for the Turkey trade, having received intelligences and advertisements from time to time that the King of Spain, grudging at the prosperity of this kingdom, had not only of late arrested all English ships, bodies, and goods in Spain, but also, maligning the quiet traffic which they used, to and in the dominions and provinces under the obedience of the Great Turk, had given orders to the captains of his galleys in the Levant to hinder the passage of all English ships, and to endeavour by their best means to intercept, take, and spoil them, their persons and goods ; they hereupon thought it their best course to set out their fleet for Turkey in such strength and ability for their defence that the purpose of their Spanish enemy might the better be prevented, and the voyage accomplished with greater security to the men and ships. For which cause, five tall and stout ships appertaining to London, and intending only a merchant's voyage, were provided and furnished with all things belonging to the seas, the names whereof were these :—

1. The *Merchant Royal*, a very brave and goodly ship, and of great report.
2. The *Toby*.
3. The *Edward Bonaventure*.
4. The *William and John*.
5. The *Susan*.

These five departing from the coast of England in the month of November, 1585, kept together as one fleet till they came as high as the isle of Sicily, within the Levant. And there, according to the order and direction of the voyage, each ship began to take leave of the rest, and to separate himself, setting his course for the particular port whereunto he was bound—one for Tripolis in Syria, another for Constantinople, the chief city of the Turk's empire, situated upon the coast of Roumelia, called of old Thracia, and the rest to those places whereunto they were privately appointed. But before they divided themselves, they altogether consulted of and about a certain and special place for their meeting again after the lading of their goods at their several ports. And in conclusion, the general agreement was to meet at Zante, an island near to the main continent of the west part of Morea, well known to all the pilots, and thought to be the fittest place for their rendezvous; concerning which meeting it was also covenanted on each side and promised that whatsoever ship of these five should first arrive at Zante, should there stay and expect the coming of the rest of the fleet for the space of twenty days. This being done, each man made his best haste, according as wind and weather would serve him, to fulfil his course and to despatch his business; and no need was there to admonish or encourage any man, seeing no time was ill-spent nor opportunity omitted on any side in the performance of each man's duty, according to his place.

It fell out that the *Toby*, which was bound for Constantinople, had made such good speed, and gotten such good weather, that she first of all the rest came back to the appointed place of Zante, and not forgetting the former conclusion, did there cast anchor, attending the arrival of the rest of the fleet, which accordingly (their business first performed) failed not to keep promise. The first next after the *Toby* was the *Royal Merchant*, which, together with the *William and John*, came from Tripolis in Syria, and arrived in Zante within the compass of the aforesaid time limited. These ships, in token of the joy on all parts conceived for their happy meeting, spared not the discharging of their ordnance, the sounding of drums and trumpets, the spreading of ensigns, with other warlike and joyful behaviours, expressing by these outward signs the inward gladness of their minds, being all as ready to join together in mutual consent to resist the cruel enemy, as now in sporting manner they made mirth and pastime among themselves. These three had not been long in the haven but the *Edward Bonaventure*, together with the *Susan* her consort, were come from Venice with their lading, the sight of whom increased the joy of the rest, and they, no less glad of the presence of the others, saluted them in most friendly and kind sort, according to the manner of the seas. And whereas some of these ships stood at that instant in some want of victuals, they were all content to stay in the port till the necessities of each ship were supplied, and nothing wanted to set out for their return.

In this port of Zante the news was fresh and current of two several armies and fleets, provided by the King of Spain, and lying in wait to intercept them: the one consisting of thirty strong galleys, so well appointed in all respects for the war that no necessary thing wanted, and this fleet hovered about the Straits of Gibraltar. The other army had in it twenty galleys, whereof some were of Sicily and some of the island of Malta, under the charge and government of John Andreas Dorea, a captain of name serving the King of Spain. These two divers and strong fleets waited and attended in the seas for none but the English ships, and no doubt made their account and sure reckoning that not a ship should escape their fury. And the opinion also of the inhabitants of the isle of Zante was, that in respect of the number of galleys in both these armies having received such strait commandment from the king, our ships and men being but few and little in comparison of them, it was a thing in human reason impossible that we should pass either without spoiling, if we resisted, or without composition at the least, and acknowledgment of duty to the Spanish king.

But it was neither the report of the attendance of these armies, nor the opinions of the people, nor anything else, that could daunt or dismay the courage of our men, who, grounding themselves upon the goodness of their cause and the promise of God to be delivered from such as without reason sought their destruction, carried resolute minds notwithstanding all impediments to adventure through the seas, and to finish their navigation maugre the beards of the Spanish soldiers. But lest they should seem too careless and too secure of their estate, and by laying the whole and entire burden of their safety upon God's Providence should foolishly presume altogether of His help, and neglect the means which was put into their hands, they failed not to enter into counsel among themselves and to deliberate advisedly for their best defence. And in the end, with general consent, the *Merchant Royal* was appointed Admiral of the fleet, and the *Toby* Vice-Admiral, by whose orders the rest promised to be directed, and each ship vowed not to break from another whatsoever extremity should fall out, but to stand to it to the death, for the honour of their country and the frustrating of the hope of the ambitious and proud enemy.

Thus in good order they left Zante and the Castle of Grecia, and committed themselves again to the seas, and proceeded in their course and voyage in quietness, without sight of any enemy till they came near to Pantalarea, an island so called betwixt Sicily and the coast of Africa; into sight whereof they came the 13th day of July, 1586. And the same day, in the morning, about seven of the clock, they descried thirteen sails in number, which were of the galleys lying in wait of purpose for them in and about that place. As soon as the English ships had spied them, they by-and-bye, according to a common order, made themselves ready for a fight, laid out their ordnance, scoured, charged, and primed them, displayed their ensigns, and left nothing undone to arm themselves thoroughly. In the meantime, the galleys more and more approached the ships, and in their banners there appeared the arms of the isles of Sicily and Malta, being all as then in the service and pay of the Spaniard. Immediately both the Admirals of the galleys sent from each of them a frigate to the Admiral of our English ships, which being come near them, the Sicilian frigate first hailed them, and demanded of them whence they were; they answered that they were of England, the arms whereof appeared in their colours. Whereupon the said frigate expostulated with them, and asked why they delayed to send or come with their captains and pursers to Don Pedro de Leiva, their General, to acknowledge their duty and obedience to him, in the name of the Spanish king, lord of those seas. Our men replied and said that they owed no such duty nor obedience to him, and therefore would acknowledge none; but commanded the frigate to depart with that answer, and not to stay longer upon her peril. With that away she went; and up came towards them the other frigate of Malta; and she in like sort hailed the Admiral, and would needs know whence they were and where they had been. Our Englishmen in the Admiral, not disdaining an answer, told them that they were of England, merchants of London, had been in Turkey, and were now returning home; and to be requited in this case, they also demanded of the frigate whence she and the rest of the galleys were. The messenger answered, "We are of Malta, and for mine own part, my name is Cavalero. These galleys are in service and pay to the King of Spain, under the conduct of Don

Pedro de Leiva, a nobleman of Spain who hath been commanded hither by the king with this present force and army of purpose to intercept you. You shall therefore," quoth he, "do well to repair to him to know his pleasure; he is a nobleman of good behaviour and courtesy, and means you no ill." The captain of the English Admiral, whose name was Master Edward Wilkinson, now one of the six masters of Her Majesty's Royal Navy, replied and said, "We purpose not at this time to make trial of Don Pedro his courtesy, whereof we are suspicious and doubtful, and not without good cause;" using withal good words to the messenger, and willing him to come aboard him, promising security and good usage, that thereby he might the better know the Spaniard's mind. Whereupon he indeed left his frigate and came aboard him, whom he entertained in friendly sort, and caused a cup of wine to be drawn for him, which he took, and began, with his cap in his hand and with reverent terms, to drink to the health of the Queen of England, speaking very honourably of Her Majesty, and giving good speeches of the courteous usage and entertainment that he himself had received in London at the time that the Duke of Alençon, brother to the late French king, was last in England. And after he had well drunk, he took his leave, speaking well of the sufficiency and goodness of our ships, and especially of the *Merchant Royal*, which he confessed to have seen before riding in the Thames near London. He was no sooner come to Don Pedro de Leiva, the Spanish General, but he was sent off again, and returned to the English Admiral, saying that the pleasure of the General was this, that either their captains, masters, and pursers should come to him with speed, or else he would set upon them, and either take them or sink them. The reply was made by Master Wilkinson aforesaid that not a man should come to him; and for the brag and threat of Don Pedro, it was not that Spanish bravado that should make them yield a jot to their hindrance, but they were as ready to make resistance as he to offer an injury. Whereupon Cavalero the messenger left bragging, and began to persuade them in quiet sort and with many words; but all his labour was to no purpose, and as his threat did nothing terrify them, so his persuasion did nothing move them to do that which he required. At the last he entreated to have the merchant of the Admiral carried by him as a messenger to the General, that so he might be satisfied and assured of their minds by one of their own company. But Master Wilkinson would agree to no such thing; although Richard Rowit, the merchant himself, seemed willing to be employed in that message, and laboured by reasonable persuasions to induce Master Wilkinson to grant it—as hoping to be an occasion by his presence and discreet answers to satisfy the General, and thereby to save the effusion of Christian blood, if it should grow to a battle. And he seemed so much the more willing to be sent, by how much deeper the oaths and protestations of this Cavalero were, that he would (as he was a true knight and a soldier) deliver him back again in safety to his company. Albeit, Master Wilkinson, who, by his long experience, had received sufficient trial of Spanish inconstancy and perjury, wished him in no case to put his life and liberty in hazard upon a Spaniard's oath; but at last, upon much entreaty, he yielded to let him go to the General, thinking indeed that good speeches and answers of reason would have contented him, whereas, otherwise, refusal to do so might peradventure have provoked the more discontentment.

Master Rowit, therefore, passing to the Spanish General, the rest of the galleys, having espied him, thought, indeed, that the English were rather determined to yield than to fight, and therefore came flocking about the frigate, every man crying out, "*Que nuevas ? que nuevas ?* Have these Englishmen yielded ?" The frigate answered, "Not so; they neither have nor purpose to yield. Only they have sent a man of their company to speak with our General." And being come to the galley wherein he was, he showed himself to Master Rowit in his armour, his guard of soldiers attending upon him, in armour also, and began to speak very proudly in this sort: "Thou Englishman, from whence is your fleet? Why stand ye aloof off? know ye not your duty to the Catholic king, whose person I here represent? Where are your bills of lading, your letters, passports, and the chief of your men? Think ye my attendance in these seas to be in vain, or my person to no purpose? Let all these things be done out of hand, as I command, upon pain of my further displeasure, and the spoil of you all." These words of the Spanish General were not so outrageously pronounced, as they were mildly answered by Master Rowit, who told him that they were all merchantmen, using traffic in honest sort, and seeking to pass quietly, if they were not urged further than reason. As for the King of Spain, he thought (for his part) that there was amity betwixt him and his Sovereign, the Queen of England, so that neither he nor his officers should go about to offer any such injury to English merchants, who, as they were far from giving offence to any man, so they would be loth to take an abuse at the hands of any, or sit down to their loss, where their ability was able to make defence. And as touching his commandment aforesaid for the acknowledging of duty in such particular sort, he told him that, where there was no duty owing there none should be performed, assuring him that their whole company and ships in general stood resolutely upon the negative, and would not yield to any such unreasonable demand, joined with such imperious and absolute manner of commanding. "Why, then," said he, "if they will neither come to yield, nor show obedience to me in the name of my king, I will either sink them or bring them to harbour; and so tell them from me." With that the frigate came away with Master Rowit, and brought him aboard to the English Admiral again, according to promise, who was no sooner entered in but by-and-bye defiance was sounded on both sides. The Spaniards hewed off the noses of the galleys, that nothing might hinder the level of the shot; and the English, on the other side, courageously prepared themselves to the combat, every man, according to his room, bent to perform his office with alacrity and diligence. In the meantime a cannon was discharged from out the Admiral of the galleys, which, being the onset of the fight, was presently answered by the English Admiral with a culverin; so the skirmish began, and grew hot and terrible. There was no powder nor shot spared, each English ship matched itself in good order against two Spanish galleys, besides the inequality of the frigates on the Spanish side. And although our men performed their parts with singular valour, according to their strength, insomuch that the enemy, as amazed therewith, would oftentimes pause and stay, and consult what was best to be done, yet they ceased not in the midst of their business to make prayer to Almighty God, the revenger of all evils and the giver of victories, that it would please Him to assist them in this good quarrel of theirs, in defending themselves against so proud a tyrant, to teach their hands to war and their fingers to fight, that the glory of the victory might redound to His name, and to the honour of true religion, which the insolent enemy sought so much to overthrow. Contrarily, the foolish Spaniards, they cried out, according to their manner, not to God, but to our Lady (as they term the Virgin Mary) saying, "Oh, Lady, help! Oh, blessed Lady, give us the victory, and the honour thereof shall be thine." Thus with blows and prayers on both sides, the fight continued furious and sharp, and doubtful a long time to which part the victory would incline, till at last the Admiral of the galleys of Sicily began to warp from the fight, and to hold up her side for fear of sinking, and after her went also two others in like case, whom all the sort of them enclosed, labouring by all their means to keep them above water, being ready by the force of English shot which they had received to perish in the seas. And what slaughter was done among the Spaniards the English were uncertain, but by a probable conjecture apparent afar off they supposed their loss was so great that they wanted men to continue the charging of their pieces; whereupon with shame and dishonour, after five hours spent in the battle, they withdrew themselves. And the English, contented in respect of their deep lading rather to continue their voyage than to follow in the chase, ceased from further blows, with the loss of only two men slain amongst them all, and another hurt in his arm, whom Master Wilkinson, with his good words and friendly promises, did so comfort that he nothing esteemed the smart of his wound, in respect of the honour of the victory and the shameful repulse of the enemy.

Thus, with dutiful thanks to the mercy of God for His gracious assistance in that danger, the

English ships proceeded in their navigation. And coming as high as Algiers, a port town upon the coast of Barbary, they made for it, of purpose to refresh themselves after their weariness, and to take in such supply of fresh water and victuals as they needed. They were no sooner entered into the port but immediately the king thereof sent a messenger to the ships to know what they were. With which messenger the chief master of every ship repaired to the king, and acquainted him not only with the state of their ships in respect of merchandise, but with the late fight which they had passed with the Spanish galleys, reporting every particular circumstance in word as it fell out in action; whereof the said king showed himself marvellous glad, entertaining them in the best sort, and promising abundant relief of all their wants; making general proclamation in the city, upon pain of death, that no man, of what degree or state soever he were, should presume either to hinder them in their affairs or to offer them any manner of injury in body or goods; by virtue whereof they despatched all things in excellent good sort with all favour and peaceableness. Only such prisoners and captives of the Spaniards as were in the city, seeing the good usage which they received, and hearing also what service they had performed against the foresaid galleys, grudged exceedingly against them, and sought as much as they could to practise some mischief against them. And one amongst the rest, seeing an Englishman alone in a certain lane of the city, came upon him suddenly, and with his knife thrust him in the side, yet made no such great wound but that it was easily recovered. The English company, hearing of it, acquainted the king of the fact; who immediately sent both for the party that had received the wound and the offender also, and caused an executioner, in the presence of himself and the English, to chastise the slave even to death, which was performed, to the end that no man should presume to commit the like part or to do anything in contempt of his royal commandment.

The English, having received this good justice at the king's hands, and all other things that they wanted or could crave for the furnishing of their ships, took their leave of him, and of the rest of their friends that were resident in Algiers, and put out to sea, looking to meet with the second army of the Spanish king, which waited for them about the mouth of the Strait of Gibraltar, which they were of necessity to pass. But coming near to the said strait, it pleased God to raise, at that instant, a very dark and misty fog, so that one ship could not discern another if it were forty paces off, by means whereof, together with the notable fair Eastern winds that then blew most fit for their course, they passed with great speed through the strait, and might have passed, with that good gale, had there been five hundred galleys to withstand them and the air never so clear for every ship to be seen. But yet the Spanish galleys had a sight of them, when they were come within three English miles of the town, and made after them with all possible haste; and although they saw that they were far out of their reach, yet in a vain fury and foolish pride, they shot off their ordnance and made a stir in the sea as if they had been in the midst of them, which vanity of theirs ministered to our men notable matter of pleasure and mirth, seeing men to fight with shadows and to take so great pains to so small purpose.

But thus it pleased God to deride and delude all the forces of that proud Spanish king, which he had provided of purpose to distress the English; who, notwithstanding, passed through both his armies—in the one, little hurt, and in the other, nothing touched, to the glory of His immortal name, the honour of our prince and country, and the just commendation of each man's service performed in that voyage.

THE UNFORTUNATE VOYAGE MADE WITH THE *JESUS*, THE *MINION*, AND FOUR OTHER SHIPS,

To the parts of Guinea and the West Indies, in the years 1567 *and* 1568. *By* MASTER JOHN HAWKINS.

THE ships departed from Plymouth the 2nd day of October, anno 1567, and had reasonable weather until the seventh day, at which time, forty leagues north from Cape Finisterre, there arose an extreme storm which continued four days, in such sort that the fleet was dispersed and all our great boats lost, and the *Jesus*, our chief ship, in such case as not thought able to serve the voyage. Whereupon in the same storm we set our course homeward, determining to give over the voyage; but the 11th day of the same month the wind changed, with fair weather, whereby we were animated to follow our enterprise, and so did, directing our course to the islands of Grand Canaries, where, according to an order before prescribed, all our ships, before dispersed, met in one of those islands, called Gomera, where we took water, and departed from thence the 4th day of November towards the coast of Guinea, and arrived at Cape Verde the 18th of November, where we landed one hundred and fifty men, (hoping to obtain some negroes;) where we got but few, and those with great hurt and damage to our men, which chiefly proceeded from their envenomed arrows; although in the beginning they seemed to be but small hurts, yet there hardly escaped any that had blood drawn of them but died in strange sort, with their mouths shut, some ten days before they died, and after their wounds were whole; where I myself had one of the greatest wounds, yet, thanks be to God, escaped. From thence we passed the time upon the coast of Guinea, searching with all diligence the rivers from Rio Grande unto Sierra Leone till the 12th of January, in which time we had not gotten together a hundred and fifty negroes: yet, notwithstanding the sickness of our men and the late time of the year commanded us away: and thus having nothing wherewith to seek the coast of the West Indies, I was with the rest of our company in consultation to go to the coast of the Myne, hoping there to have obtained some gold for our wares, and thereby to have defrayed our charge. But even in that present instant there came to us a negro sent from a king oppressed by other kings, his neighbours, desiring our aid, with promise that as many negroes as by these wars might be obtained, as well of his part as of ours, should be at our pleasure. Whereupon we concluded to give aid, and sent one hundred and twenty of our men, which the 15th of January assaulted a town of the negroes of our allies' adversaries which had in it 8,000 inhabitants, and very strongly impaled and fenced after their manner, but it was so well defended that our men prevailed not, but lost six men, and forty hurt, so that our men sent forthwith to me for more help; whereupon, considering that the good success of this enterprise might highly further the commodity of our voyage, I went myself, and with the help of the king of our side assaulted the town, both by land and sea, and very hardly with fire (their houses being covered with dry palm leaves) obtained the town, and put the inhabitants to flight, where we took 250 persons, men, women, and children, and by our friend the king of our side there were taken 600 prisoners, whereof we hoped to have our choice, but the negro (in which nation is seldom or never found truth) meant nothing less; for that night he removed his camp and prisoners, so that we were fain to content us with those few which we had gotten ourselves.

Now had we obtained between four and five hundred negroes, wherewith we thought it somewhat reasonable to seek the coast of the West

Indies, and there, for our negroes, and other our merchandise, we hoped to obtain whereof to countervail our charges with some gains, whereunto we proceeded with all diligence, furnished our watering, took fuel, and departed the coast of Guinea, the third of February, continuing at the sea with a passage more hard than before hath been accustomed, till the 27th day of March, which day we had sight of an island, called Dominique, upon the coast of the West Indies, in fourteen degrees: from thence we coasted from place to place, making our traffic with the Spaniards as we might, somewhat hardly, because the king had straitly commanded all his governors in those parts by no means to suffer any trade to be made with us; notwithstanding we had reasonable trade, and courteous entertainment, from the Isle of Marguerite and Cartagena, without anything greatly worth the noting, saving at Capo de la Vela, in a town called Rio de la Hacha, from whence come all the pearls. The treasurer who had the charge there would by no means agree to any trade, or suffer us to take water. He had fortified his town with divers bulwarks in all places where it might be entered, and furnished himself with a hundred harquebusiers, so that he thought by famine to have enforced us to have put on land our negroes, of which purpose he had not greatly failed unless we had by force entered the town; which (after we could by no means obtain his favour) we were enforced to do, and so with two hundred men brake in upon their bulwarks, and entered the town with the loss only of eleven men of our parts, and no hurt done to the Spaniards, because after their volley of shot discharged, they all fled.

Thus having the town, with some circumstance, as partly by the Spaniards' desire of negroes, and partly by friendship of the treasurer, we obtained a secret trade; whereupon the Spaniards resorted to us by night, and bought of us to the number of two hundred negroes: in all other places where we traded the Spaniards inhabitants were glad of us, and traded willingly.

At Cartagena, the last town we thought to have seen on the coast, we could by no means obtain to deal with any Spaniard, the governor was so strait, and because our trade was so near finished, we thought not good either to adventure any landing or to detract further time, but in peace departed from thence the 24th of July, hoping to have escaped the time of their storms, which then soon after began to reign, the which they call *Furicanos;* but passing by the west end of Cuba, towards the coast of Florida, there happened to us, the twelfth day of August, an extreme storm, which continued by the space of four days, which so beat the *Jesus*, that we cut down all her higher buildings; her rudder also was sore shaken, and, withal, was in so extreme a leak, that we were rather upon the point to leave her than to keep her any longer; yet, hoping to bring all to good pass, sought the coast of Florida, where we found no place nor haven for our ships, because of the shallowness of the coast. Thus, being in greater despair, and taken with a new storm, which continued other three days, we were enforced to take for our succour the port which serveth the city of Mexico, called St. John de Ullua, which standeth in nineteen degrees, in seeking of which port we took in our way three ships, which carried passengers to the number of one hundred, which passengers we hoped should be a means to us the better to obtain victuals for our money and a quiet place for the repairing of our fleet. Shortly after this, the sixteenth of September, we entered the port of St. John de Ullua, and in our entry, the Spaniards thinking us to be the fleet of Spain, the chief officers of the country came aboard us, which, being deceived of their expectation, were greatly dismayed, but immediately, when they saw our demand was nothing but victuals, were recomforted. I found also in the same port twelve ships, which had in them, by the report, 200,000 livres in gold and silver, all which (being in my possession with the King's island, as also the passengers before in my way thitherward stayed) I set at liberty, without the taking from them the weight of a groat; only, because I would not be delayed of my despatch, I stayed two men of estimation, and sent post immediately to Mexico, which was two hundred miles from us, to the presidents and Council there, showing them of our arrival there by the force of weather, and the necessity of the repair of our ship and victuals, which wants we required, as friends to King Philip, to be furnished of for our money, and that the presidents in council there should, with all convenient speed, take order that at the arrival of the Spanish fleet, which was daily looked for, there might no cause of quarrel rise between us and them, but, for the better maintenance of amity, their commandment might be had in that behalf. This message being sent away the 16th day of September, at night, being the very day of our arrival, in the next morning, which was the sixteenth day of the same month, we saw open of the haven thirteen great ships, and understanding them to be the fleet of Spain, I sent immediately to advertise the general of the fleet of my being there, doing him to understand that, before I would suffer them to enter the port, there should be some order of conditions pass between us for our safe being there and maintenance of peace. Now, it is to be understood that this port is a little island of stones, not three feet above the water in the highest place, and but a bow-shot of length any way. This island standeth from the mainland two bow shots or more. Also it is to be understood that there is not in all this coast any other place for ships to arrive in safety, because the north wind hath there such violence, that, unless the ships be very safely moored, with their anchors fastened upon this island, there is no remedy for these north winds but death; also, the place of the haven was so little, that of necessity the ships must ride one aboard the other, so that we could not give place to them nor they to us; and here I began to bewail the which after followed: "For now," said I, "I am in two dangers, and forced to receive the one of them." That was, either I must have kept out the fleet from entering the port (the which, with God's help, I was very well able to do), or else suffer them to enter in with their accustomed treason, which they never fail to execute where they may have opportunity, or circumvent it by any means. If I had kept them out, then had there been present shipwreck of all the fleet, which amounted in value to six millions, which was in value of our money 1,800,000 livres, which I considered I was not able to answer, fearing the Queen's Majesty's indignation in so weighty a matter. Thus with myself revolving the doubts, I thought rather better to abide the jutt of the uncertainty than the certainty. The uncertain doubt was their treason, which by good policy I hoped might be prevented; and therefore, as choosing the least mischief, I proceeded to conditions. Now was our first messenger come and returned from the fleet with report of the arrival of a Viceroy, so that he had authority, both in all this province of Mexico (otherwise called Nova Hispania) and in the sea, who sent us word that we should send our conditions, which of his part should (for the better maintenance of amity between the princes) be both favourably granted and faithfully performed, with many fair words how, passing the coast of the Indies, he had understood of our honest behaviour towards the inhabitants, where we had to do as well elsewhere as in the same port, the which I let pass, thus following our demand. We required victual for our money, and licence to sell as much ware as might furnish our wants, and that there might be of either part twelve gentlemen as hostage for the maintenance of peace, and that the island, for our better safety, might be in our own possession during our abode there, and such ordnance as was planted in the same island, which was eleven pieces of brass, and that no Spaniard might land in the island with any kind of weapon.

These conditions at the first he somewhat misliked—chiefly the guard of the island to be in our own keeping, which, if they had had, we had soon known our fate; for with the first north wind they had cut our cables, and our ships had gone ashore; but in the end he concluded to our request, bringing the twelve hostages to ten, which with all speed on either part were received, with a writing from the Viceroy, signed with his hand and sealed with his seal, of all the conditions concluded, and forthwith a trumpet blown, with commandment that none of either part should inviolate the peace upon pain of death; and, further, it was concluded that the two generals of the fleet should meet, and give faith each to other for the performance of the promises, which was so done.

Thus, at the end of three days, all was concluded, and the fleet entered the port, saluting one another as the manner of the sea doth require. Thus, as I said before, Thursday we entered the port, Friday we saw the fleet, and on Monday, at night, they entered the port; then we laboured two days, placing the English ships by themselves, and the Spanish ships by themselves, the captains of each part, and inferior men of their parts, promising great amity of all sides; which, even as with all fidelity was meant of our part, though the Spanish meant nothing less of their parts, but from the mainland had furnished themselves with a supply of men to the number of one thousand, and meant the next Thursday, being the 23rd of September, at dinner-time, to set upon us of all sides. The same Thursday, the treason being at hand, some appearance showed, as shifting of weapons from ship to ship, planting and bending of ordnance from the ship to the island where our men were, passing to and fro of companies of men more than required for their necessary business, and many other ill likelihoods, which caused us to have a vehement suspicion, and therewithal sent to the Viceroy to inquire what was meant by it, which sent immediately straight commandment to unplant all things suspicious, and also sent word that he, in the faith of a Viceroy, would be our defence from all villainies. Yet we, not being satisfied with this answer, because we suspected a great number of men to be hid in a great ship of nine hundred tons, which was moored next unto the *Minion*, sent again unto the Viceroy the master of the *Jesus*, which had the Spanish tongue, and required to be satisfied if any such thing were or not; on which the Viceroy, seeing that the treason must be discovered, forthwith stayed our master, blew the trumpet, and of all sides set upon us. Our men which were on guard ashore, being stricken with sudden fear, gave place, fled, and sought to recover succour of the ships; the Spaniards, being before provided for the purpose, landed in all places in multitudes from their ships, which they could easily do without boats, and slew all our men ashore without mercy, a few of them escaping aboard the *Jesus*. The great ship which had, by the estimation, three hundred men placed in her secretly, immediately fell aboard the *Minion*, which, by God's appointment, in the time of the suspicion we had, which was only one half-hour, the *Minion* was made ready to avoid, and so, loosing her headfasts, and hailing away by the sternfasts, she was gotten out; thus, with God's help, she defended the violence of the first brunt of these three hundred men. The *Minion* being passed out, they came aboard the *Jesus*, which also, with very much ado and the loss of many of our men, were defended and kept out. Then were there also two other ships that assaulted the *Jesus* at the same instant, so that she had hard work getting loose; but yet, with some time, we had cut our headfasts, and gotten out by the sternfasts. Now, when the *Jesus* and the *Minion* were gotten two ship-lengths from the Spanish fleet, the fight began hot on all sides, so that within one hour the admiral of the Spaniards was supposed to be sunk, their vice-admiral burned, and one other of their principal ships supposed to be sunk, so that the ships were little to annoy us.

Then is it to be understood that all the ordnance upon the island was in the Spaniards' hands, which did us so great annoyance that it cut all the masts and yards of the *Jesus* in such sort, that there was no hope to carry her away; also it sank our small ships, whereupon we determined to place the *Jesus* on that side of the *Minion*, that she might abide all the battery from the land, and so be a defence for the *Minion* till night, and then to take such relief of victual and other necessaries from the *Jesus* as the time would suffer us, and to leave her. As we were thus determining, and had placed the *Minion* from the shot of the land, suddenly the Spaniards had fired two great ships which were coming directly to us, and having no means to avoid the fire, it bred among our men a marvellous fear, so that some said, "Let us depart with the *Minion*," others said, "Let us see whether the wind will carry the fire from us." But to be short, the *Minion's* men, which had always their sails in a readiness, thought to make sure work, and so without either consent of the captain or master, cut their sail, so that very hardly I was received into the *Minion*.

The most part of the men that were left alive in the *Jesus* made shift and followed the *Minion* in a small boat, the rest, which the little boat was not able to receive, were enforced to abide the mercy of the Spaniards (which I doubt was very little); so with the *Minion* only, and the *Judith* (a small barque of fifty tons) we escaped, which barque the same night forsook us in our great misery. We were now removed with the *Minion* from the Spanish ships two bow-shots, and there rode all that night. The next morning we recovered an island a mile from the Spaniards, where there took us a north wind, and being left only with two anchors and two cables (for in this conflict we lost three cables and two anchors), we thought always upon death, which ever was present, but God preserved us to a longer time.

The weather waxed reasonable, and the Saturday

we set sail, and having a great number of men and little victual, our hope of life waxed less and less. Some desired to yield to the Spaniards, some rather desired to obtain a place where they might give themselves to the infidels; and some had rather abide, with a little pittance, the mercy of God at sea. So thus, with many sorrowful hearts, we wandered in an unknown sea by the space of fourteen days, till hunger enforced us to seek the land; for hides were thought very good meat; rats, cats, mice, and dogs, none escaped that might be gotten; parrots and monkeys, that were had in great prize, were thought there very profitable if they served the turn of one dinner. Thus in the end, on the 8th day of October, we came to the land in the bottom of the same bay of Mexico, in twenty-three degrees and a half, where we hoped to have found habitations of the Spaniards, relief of victuals, and place for the repair of our ship, which was so sore beaten with shot from our enemies, and bruised with shooting of our own ordnance, that our weary and weak arms were scarce able to defend and keep out the water. But all things happened to the contrary, for we found neither people, victual, nor haven of relief, but a place where, having fair weather, with some peril we might land a boat. Our people, being forced with hunger, desired to be set aland, whereunto I concluded.

And such as were willing to land I put apart, and such as were desirous to go homewards I put apart, so that they were indifferently parted, a hundred of one side and a hundred of the other side. These hundred men we set on land with all diligence, in this little place aforesaid, which being landed, we determined there to refresh our water, and so with our little remain of victuals to take the sea.

The next day, having on land with me fifty of our hundred men that remained, for the speedier preparing of our water aboard, there arose an extreme storm, so that in three days we could by no means repair our ships. The ship also was in such peril that every hour we looked for shipwreck.

But yet God again had mercy on us, and sent fair weather. We got aboard our water, and departed the 16th day of October, after which day we had fair and properous weather till the 16th day of November, which day, God be praised, we were clear from the coast of the Indians and out of the channel and gulf of Bahama, which is between the cape of Florida and the islands of Cuba. After this, growing near to the cold country, our men, being oppressed with famine, died continually, and they that were left grew into such weakness that we were scarcely able to manœuvre our ship, and the wind being always ill for us to recover England, determined to go to Galicia, in Spain, with intent there to relieve our company and other extreme wants. And being arrived the last day of December, in a place near unto Vigo, called Pontevedra, our men, with excess of fresh meat, grew into miserable diseases, and died a great part of them. This matter was borne out as long as it might be, but in the end, although there was none of our men suffered to go on land, yet by access of the Spaniards our feebleness was known to them. Whereupon they ceased not to seek by all means to betray us, but with all speed possible we departed to Vigo, where we had some help of certain English ships, and twelve fresh men, wherewith we repaired our wants as we might, and departing the 20th day of January, 1568, arrived in Mount's Bay in Cornwall the 25th of the same month, praised be God therefore.

If all the misery and troublesome affairs of this sorrowful voyage should be perfectly and thoroughly written, there should need a painful man with his pen, and as great time as he had that wrote the "Lives and Deaths of the Martyrs."

JOHN HAWKINS.

A DISCOURSE WRITTEN BY ONE MILES PHILLIPS,

Englishman, one of the company put ashore in the West Indies by Master John Hawkins in the year 1568, containing many special things of that country and of the Spanish Government, but specially of their cruelties used to our Englishmen, and amongst the rest, to himself, for the space of fifteen or sixteen years together, until by good and happy means he was delivered from their bloody hands, and returned to his own country. Anno 1582.

THE FIRST CHAPTER.

Wherein is shown the day and time of our departure from the coast of England, with the number and names of the ships, their captains and masters, and of our traffic and dealing upon the coast of Africa.

UPON Monday, being the 2nd of October, 1567, the weather being reasonable fair, our General, Master John Hawkins, having commanded all his captains and masters to be in a readiness to make sail with him, he himself being embarked in the *Jesus*, whereof was appointed for master Robert Barret, hoisted sail and departed from Plymouth upon his intended voyage for the parts of Africa and America, being accompanied with five other sail of ships, as namely the *Minion*, wherein went for captain Master John Hampton, and John Garret, master. The *William and John*, wherein was Captain Thomas Bolton, and James Raunce, master. The *Judith*, in whom was Captain Master Francis Drake, now Knight, and the *Angel*, whose master, as also the captain and master of the *Swallow*, I now remember not. And so sailing in company together upon our voyage until the 10th of the same month, an extreme storm then took us near unto Cape Finisterre, which lasted for the space of four days, and so separated our ships that we had lost one another, and our General, finding the *Jesus* to be but in ill case, was in mind to give over the voyage and to return home. Howbeit, the eleventh of the same month, the seas waxing calm and the wind coming fair, he altered his purpose, and held on the former intended voyage; and so coming to the island of Gomera, being one of the islands of the Canaries, where, according to an order before appointed, we met with all our ships which were before dispersed. We then took in fresh water and departed from thence the 4th of November, and holding on our course, upon the 18th day of the same month we came to an anchor upon the coast of Africa, at Cape Verde, in twelve fathoms of water, and here our General landed certain of our men, to the number of 160 or thereabouts, seeking to take some negroes. And they, going up into the country for the space of six miles, were encountered with a great number of the negroes, who with their envenomed arrows did hurt a great number of our men, so that they were enforced to retire to the ships, in which conflict they recovered but a few negroes; and of these our men which were hurt with their envenomed arrows, there died to the number of seven or eight in very strange manner, with their mouths shut, so that we were forced to put sticks and other things into their mouths to keep them open; and so afterwards passing the time upon the coast of Guinea, until the 12th of January, we obtained by that time the number of one hundred and fifty negroes. And being ready to depart from the sea coast, there was a negro sent as an ambassador to our General, from a king of the negroes, which was oppressed with other kings, his bordering kings, desiring our General to grant him succour and aid against those his enemies, which our General granted unto, and went himself in person on land with the number of 200 of our men, or thereabouts, and the said king which had requested our aid, did join his force with ours, so that thereby our General assaulted and set fire upon a town of the said king his enemies, in which there was at the least the number of eight or ten thousand negroes, and they, perceiving that they were not able to make any resistance, sought by flight to save themselves, in which their flight there were taken prisoners to the number of eight or nine hundred, which our General ought to have had for his share; howbeit the negro king, which requested our aid, falsifying his word and promise, secretly in the night conveyed himself away with as many prisoners as he had in his custody; but our General, notwithstanding finding himself to have now very near the number of 500 negroes, thought it best without longer abode to depart with them and such merchandise as he had from the coast of Africa towards the West Indies, and therefore commanded with all diligence to take in fresh water and fuel, and so with speed to prepare to depart. Howbeit, before we departed from thence, in a storm that we had, we lost one of our ships, namely, the *William and John*, of which ship and her people we heard no tidings during the time of our voyage.

THE SECOND CHAPTER.

Wherein is showed the day and time of our departure from the coast of Africa, with the day and time of our arrival in the West Indies, also of our trade and traffic there, and also of the great cruelty that the Spaniards used towards us, by the Viceroy his direction and appointment, falsifying his faith and promise given, and seeking to have entrapped us.

ALL things being made in a readiness at our General his appointment, upon the 3rd day of February, 1568, we departed from the coast of Africa, having the weather somewhat tempestuous, which made our passage the more hard, and sailing so for the space of twenty-five days, upon the 27th March, 1568, we came in sight of an island called Dominique, upon the coast of America, in the West Indies, situated in fourteen degrees of latitude, and two hundred and twenty-two of longitude. From thence our General coasted from place to place, ever making traffic with the Spaniards and Indians, as he might, which was somewhat hardly obtained, for that the king had straitly charged all his governors in those parts not to trade with any. Yet notwithstanding, during the months of April and May, our General had reasonable trade and traffic, and courteous entertainment in sundry places, as at Marguerite, Corassoa, and elsewhere, until we came to Cape de la Vela, and Rio de la Hacha (a place from whence all the pearls do come). The governor there would not by any means permit us to have any trade or traffic, nor yet suffer us to take in fresh water; by means whereof our General, for the avoiding of famine and thirst, about the beginning of June was enforced to land 200 of our men, and so by main force and strength to obtain that which by no fair means he could procure; and so recovering the town with the loss of two of our men, there was a secret and peaceable trade admitted, and the Spaniards came in by night, and bought of our negroes to the number of 200 and upwards, and of our other merchandise also. From thence we departed for Cartagena, where the governor was so strait that we could not obtain any traffic there, and so for that our trade was near finished, our General thought it best to depart from thence the rather for the avoiding of certain dangerous storms called the huricanoes, which accustomed to begin there about that time of the year, and so the 24th of July, 1568, we departed from thence, directing our course north, leaving the islands of Cuba upon our right hand, to the eastward of us, and so sailing towards Florida, upon the 12th of August an extreme tempest arose, which dured for the space of eight days, in which our ships were most dangerously tossed, and beaten hither and thither, so that we were in continual fear to be drowned, by reason of the shallowness of the coast, and in the end we were constrained to flee for succour to the port of St. John de Ullua, or Vera Cruz, situated in nineteen degrees of latitude, and in two hundred and seventy-nine degrees of longitude, which is the port that serveth for the city of Mexico. In our seeking to recover this port our General met by the way three small ships that carried passengers, which he took with him, and so the 16th of September, 1568, we entered the said port of St. John de Ullua. The Spaniards there, supposing us to have been the King of Spain's fleet, the chief officers of the country thereabouts came presently aboard our General, where perceiving themselves to have made an unwise adventure, they were in great fear to have been taken and stayed; howbeit our General did use them all very courteously. In the said port there were twelve ships, which by report had in them in treasure, to the value of two hundred thousand pounds, all which being in our General his power, and at his devotion, he did freely set at liberty, as also the passengers which he had before stayed, not taking from any of them all the value of one groat, only we stayed two men of credit and account, the one named Don Lorenzo de Alva, and the other Don Pedro de Revera, and presently our General sent to the Viceroy to Mexico, which was threescore leagues off, certifying him of our arrival there by force of weather, desiring that forasmuch as our Queen, his Sovereign, was the King of Spain his loving sister and friend, that therefore he would, considering our necessities and wants, furnish us with victuals for our navy, and quietly to suffer us to repair and amend our ships. And furthermore that at the arrival of the Spanish fleet, which was there daily expected and looked for, to the end that there might no quarrel arise between them and our General and his company for the breach of amity, he humbly requested of his excellency that there might in this behalf some special order be taken. This message was sent away the 16th of September, 1568, it being the very day of our arrival there. The next morning, being the 17th of the same month, we descried thirteen sail of great ships; and after that our General understood that it was the King of Spain's fleet then looked for, he presently sent to advertise the General hereof of our being in the said port, and giving him further to understand, that before he should enter there into that harbour, it was requisite that there should pass between the two

Generals some orders and conditions, to be observed on either part, for the better contriving of peace between them and theirs, according to our General's request made unto the Viceroy. And at this instant our General was in a great perplexity of mind, considering with himself that if he should keep out that fleet from entering into the port, a thing which he was very well able to do with the help of God, then should that fleet be in danger of present shipwreck and loss of all their substance, which amounted unto the value of one million and eight hundred thousand crowns. Again, he saw that if he suffered them to enter, he was assured they would practise all manner of means to betray him and his, and on the other side the haven was so little, that the other fleet entering, the ships were to ride one hard aboard of another; also he saw that if their fleet should perish by his keeping them out, as of necessity they must if he should have done so, then stood he in great fear of the Queen our Sovereign's displeasure; in so weighty a cause, therefore, did he choose the least evil, which was to suffer them to enter under assurance, and so to stand upon his guard, and to defend himself and his from their treasons, which we were all assured they would practise, and so the messenger being returned from Don Martine de Henriquez, the new

Viceroy, who came in the same fleet, and had sufficient authority to command in all cases both by sea and land in this province of Mexico or New Spain, did certify our General, that for the better maintenance of amity between the King of Spain and our Sovereign, all our requests should be both favourably granted and faithfully performed; signifying further that he heard and understood of the honest and friendly dealing of our General towards the King of Spain's subjects in all places where he had been, as also in the said port; so that to be brief our requests were articled and set down in writing, viz.—

1. The first was that we might have victuals for our money and license to sell as much wares as might suffice to furnish our wants.

2. The second, that we might be suffered peaceably to repair our ships.

3. The third, that the island might be in our possession during the time of our abode there, in which island our General, for the better safety of him and his, had already planted and placed certain ordnance, which were eleven pieces of brass; therefore he required that the same might so continue, and that no Spaniard should come to land in the said island having or wearing any kind of weapon about him.

4. The fourth and the last, that for the better and more sure performance and maintenance of peace, and of all the conditions, there might twelve gentlemen of credit be delivered of either part as hostages.

These conditions were concluded and agreed upon in writing by the Viceroy and signed with his hand, and sealed with his seal, and ten hostages upon either part were received. And farther, it was concluded that the two Generals should meet and give faith each to other for the performance of the promises. All which being done, the same was proclaimed by the sound of a trumpet, and commandment was given that none of either part should violate or break the peace upon pain of death. Thus, at the end of three days all was concluded, and the fleet entered the port, the ships saluting each other as the manner of the seas doth require. The morrow after being Friday, we laboured on all sides in placing the English ships by themselves and the Spanish ships by themselves; the captains and inferior persons of either part offering and showing great courtesy one to another, and promising great amity upon all sides. Howbeit, as the sequel showed, the Spaniards meant nothing less upon their parts. For the Viceroy and the governor thereabout had secretly on land assembled to the number of one thousand chosen men, and well appointed, meaning the next Thursday, being the 24th of September, at dinner time to assault us, and set upon us on all sides. But before I go any further, I think it not amiss briefly to describe the manner of the island as it then was, and the force and strength that it is now of. For the Spaniards, since the time of our General's being there, for the better fortifying of the same place, have upon the same island built a fair castle and bulwark very well fortified; this port was then, at our being there, a little island of stones, not past three foot above water in the highest place, and not past a bow's shot over any way at the most, and it standeth from the mainland two bow-shots or more, and there is not in all this coast any other place for ships safely to arrive at; also the north winds in this coast are of great violence and force, and unless the ships be safely moored in, with their anchors fastened in this island, there is no remedy, but present destruction and shipwreck. All this our General, wisely foreseeing, did provide that he would have the said island in his custody, or else the Spaniards might at their pleasure have but cut our cables, and so with the first north wind that blew we had had our passport, for our ships had gone ashore. But to return to the matter. The time approaching that their treason must be put in practice, the same Thursday morning, some appearance thereof began to show itself, as shifting of weapons from ship to ship, and planting and bending their ordnance against our men that warded upon the land with great repair of people; which apparent shows of breach of the Viceroy's faith caused our General to send one to the Viceroy to inquire of him what was meant thereby, who presently sent and gave order that the ordnance aforesaid and other things of suspicion should be removed, returning answer to our General in the faith of a Viceroy that he would be our defence and safety from all villainous treachery. This was upon Thursday, in the morning. Our General not being therewith satisfied, seeing they had secretly conveyed a great number of men aboard a great hulk or ship of theirs of nine hundred tons, which ship rode hard by the *Minion*, he sent again to the Viceroy Robert Barret, the master of the *Jesus*—a man that could speak the Spanish tongue very well, and required that those men might be unshipped again which were in that great hulk. The Viceroy then perceiving that their treason was thoroughly espied, stayed our master and sounded the trumpet, and gave order that his people should upon all sides charge upon our men which warded on shore and elsewhere, which struck such a maze and sudden fear among us, that many gave place and sought to recover our ships for the safety of themselves. The Spaniards, which secretly were hid in ambush on land, were quickly conveyed over to the island in their long boats, and so coming to the island they slew all our men that they could meet with without any mercy. The *Minion*—which had somewhat before prepared herself to avoid the danger—hailed away, and abode the first brunt of the three hundred men that were in the great hulk; then they sought to fall aboard the *Jesus*, where was a cruel fight, and many of our men slain; but yet our men defended themselves, and kept them out: so the *Jesus* also got loose, and, joining with the *Minion*, the fight waxed hot upon all sides; but they having won and got our ordnance on shore, did greatly annoy us. In this fight there were two great ships of the Spaniards sunk and one burnt, so that with their ships they were not able to harm us; but from the shore they beat us cruelly with our own ordnance in such sort that the *Jesus* was very sore spoiled, and suddenly the Spaniards, having fired two great ships of their own, came directly against us, which bred among our men a marvellous fear. Howbeit, the *Minion*, which had made her sails ready, shifted for herself without cnosent of the General, captain, or master, so that very hardly our General could be received into the *Minion;* the most of our men that were in the *Jesus* shifted for themselves, and followed the *Minion* in the boat, and those which that small boat was not able to receive were most cruelly slain by the Spaniards. Of our ships none escaped save the *Minion* and the *Judith*, and all such of our men as were not in them were enforced to abide the tyrannous cruelty of the Spaniards. For it is a certain truth, that whereas they had taken certain of our men at shore, they took and hung them up by the arms upon high posts until the blood burst out of their fingers' ends; of which men so used there is one Copstowe and certain others yet alive, who, through the merciful Providence of the Almighty, were long since arrived here at home in England, carrying still about with them (and shall to their graves) the marks and tokens of those their inhuman and more than barbarous cruel dealing.

THE THIRD CHAPTER.

Wherein is showed how that, after we were escaped from the Spaniards, we were like to perish with famine at the sea, and how our General, for the avoiding thereof, was constrained to put half of his men on land, and what miseries we after that sustained amongst the savage people, and how we fell again into the hands of the Spaniards.

AFTER that the Viceroy, Don Martin Henriques, had thus contrary to his faith and promise most cruelly dealt with our General, Master Hawkins, at St. John de Ullua, where most of his men were by the Spaniards slain and drowned, and all his ships sunk and burnt, saving the *Minion* and the *Judith*, which was a small barque of fifty tons, wherein was then captain Master Francis Drake aforesaid; the same night the said barque was lost us, we being in great necessity and enforced to move with the *Minion* two bow-shots from the Spanish fleet, where we anchored all that night; and the next morning we weighed anchor and recovered an island a mile from the Spaniards, where a storm took us with a north wind, in which we were greatly distressed, having but two cables and two anchors left; for in the conflict before we had lost three cables and two anchors. The morrow after, the storm being ceased and the weather fair, we weighed and set sail, being many men in number and but small store of victuals to suffice us for any long time; by means whereof we were in despair and fear that we should perish through famine, so that some were in mind to yield themselves to the mercy of the Spaniards, other some to the savages or infidels, and wandering thus certain days in these unknown seas, hunger constrained us to eat hides, cats and dogs, mice, rats, parrots, and monkeys, to be short, our hunger was so great that we thought it savoury and sweet whatsoever we could get to eat.

And on the 8th of October we came to land again, in the bottom of the Bay of Mexico, where we hoped to have found some inhabitants, that we might have had some relief of victuals and a place where to repair our ship, which was so greatly bruised that we were scarce able, with our weary arms, to keep out the water. Being thus oppressed, by famine on the one side and danger of drowning on the other, not knowing where to find relief, we began to be in wonderful despair. And we were of many minds, amongst whom there were a great many that did desire our General to set them on land, making their choice rather to submit themselves to the mercy of the savages or infidels than longer to hazard themselves at sea, where they very well saw that if they should all remain together, if they perished not by drowning, yet hunger would enforce them, in the end, to eat one another. To which request our General did very willingly agree, considering with himself that it was necessary for him to lessen his number, both for the safety of himself and the rest. And, thereupon, being resolved to set half his people on shore that he had then left alive, it was a world to see how suddenly men's minds were altered, for they which a little before desired to be set on land were now of another mind, and requested rather to stay, by means whereof our General was enforced, for the more contenting of all men's minds, and to take away all occasions of offence, to take this order: first he made choice of such persons of service and account as were needful to stay, and that being done, of those which were willing to go, he appointed such as he thought might be best spared, and presently appointed that by the boat they should be set on shore, our General promising us that the next year he would either come himself or else send to fetch us home. Here, again, it would have caused any stony heart to have relented to hear the pitiful moan that many did make, and how loth they were to depart. The weather was then somewhat stormy and tempestuous, and therefore we were in great danger, yet, notwithstanding there was no remedy, but we that were appointed to go away must of necessity do so. Howbeit, those that went in the first boat were safely set ashore, but of them which went in the second boat, of which number I myself was one, the seas wrought so high that we could not attain to the shore, and therefore we were constrained— through the cruel dealing of John Hampton, captain of the *Minion*, and John Sanders, boatswain of the *Jesus*, and Thomas Pollard, his mate —to leap out of the boat into the main sea, having more than a mile to shore, and so to shift for ourselves, and either to sink or swim. And of those that so were, as it were, thrown out and compelled to leap into the sea, there were two drowned, which were of Captain Bland's men.

In the evening of the same day—it being Monday, the 8th of October, 1568—when we were all come to shore, we found fresh water, whereof some of our men drank so much that they had almost cast themselves away, for we could scarce get life in them for the space of two or three hours after. Other some were so cruelly swollen—what with the drinking in of the salt water, and what with the eating of the fruit which we found on land, having a stone in it much like an almond, which fruit is called capule—that they were all in very ill case, so that we were, in a manner, all of us, both feeble, weak, and faint.

The next morning—it being Tuesday, the 9th of October—we thought it best to travel along by the sea coast, to seek out some place of habitation—whether they were Christians or savages we were indifferent—so that we might have wherewithal to sustain our hungry bodies; and so departing from a hill where we had rested all night, not having any dry thread about us, for those that were not wet being thrown into the sea were thoroughly wet with rain, for all the night it rained cruelly. As we went from the hill, and were come into the plain, we were greatly troubled to pass for the grass and woods, that grew there higher than any man. On the left hand we had the sea, and upon the right hand great woods, so that of necessity we must needs pass on our way westward through those marshes, and going thus, suddenly we were assaulted by the Indians, a warlike kind of people, which are in a manner as cannibals, although they do not feed upon man's flesh as cannibals do.

These people are called Chichemici, and they used to wear their hair long, even down to their knees; they do also colour their faces green, yellow, red, and blue, which maketh them to seem very ugly and terrible to behold. These people do keep wars against the Spaniards, of whom they have been oftentimes very cruelly handled: for with the Spaniards there is no mercy. They, perceiving us at our first coming on land, supposed us to have been their enemies the bordering Spaniards; and having, by their forerunners, descried what number we were, and how feeble and weak, without armour or weapon, they suddenly, according to their accustomed manner when they encounter with any people in warlike sort, raised a terrible and huge cry, and so came running fiercely upon us, shooting off their arrows as thick as hail, unto whose mercy we were constrained to yield, not having amongst us any kind of armour, nor yet weapon, saving one caliver and two old rusty swords, whereby to make any resistance or to save ourselves; which, when they perceived that we sought not any other than favour and mercy at their hands, and that we were not their enemies the Spaniards, they had compassion on us, and came and caused us all to sit down. And when they had a while surveyed, and taken a perfect view of us, they came to all such as had any coloured clothes amongst us, and those they did strip stark naked, and took their clothes away with them; but they that were apparelled in black they did not meddle withal, and so went their ways and left us, without doing us any further hurt, only in the first brunt they killed eight of our men. And at our departure they, perceiving in what weak case we were, pointed us with their hands which way we should go to come to a town of the Spaniards, which, as we afterwards perceived, was not past ten leagues from thence, using these words: "*Tampeco, tampeco, Christiano, tampeco, Christiano,*" which is as much (we think) as to say in English, "Go that way, and you shall find the Christians." The weapons that they use are no other but bows and arrows, and their aim is so good that they very seldom miss to hit anything that they shoot at. Shortly after they had left us stripped, as aforesaid, we thought it best to divide ourselves into two companies, and so, being separated, half of us went under the leading one of Anthony Goddard, who is yet alive, and dwelleth at this instant in the town of Plymouth, whom before we chose to be captain over us all. And those that went under his leading, of which number I, Miles Phillips, was one, travelled westward—that way which the Indians with their hands had before pointed us to go. The other half went under the leading of one John Hooper, whom they did choose for their captain, and with the company that went with him David Ingram was one, and they took their way and travelled northward. And shortly after, within the space of two days, they were again encountered by the savage people, and their Captain Hooper and two more of his company were slain. Then again they divided themselves; and some held on their way still northward, and other some, knowing that we were gone westward, sought to meet with us again, as, in truth, there was about the number of five-and-twenty or six-and-twenty of them that met with us in the space of four days again. And then we began to reckon amongst ourselves how many we were that were set on shore, and we found the number to be an hundred and fourteen, whereof two were drowned in the sea and eight were slain at the first encounter, so that there remained an hundred and four, of which five-and-twenty went westward with us, and two-and-fifty to the north with Hooper and Ingram; and, as Ingram since has often told me, there were not past three of their company slain, and there were but five-and-twenty of them that came again to us, so that of the company that went northward there is yet lacking, and not certainly heard of, the number of three-and-twenty men. And verily I do think that there are of them yet alive and married in the said country, at Sibola, as hereafter I do purpose (God willing) to discourse of more particularly, with the reasons and causes that make me so to think of them that were lacking, which were with David Ingram, Twide, Browne, and sundry others, whose names we could not remember. And being thus met again together we travelled on still westward, sometimes through such thick woods that we were enforced with cudgels to break away the brambles and bushes from tearing our naked bodies; other sometimes we should travel through the plains in such high grass that we could scarce see one another. And as we passed in some places we should have of our men slain, and fall down suddenly, being stricken by the Indians, which stood behind trees and bushes, in secret places, and so killed our men as they went by; for we went scatteringly in seeking of fruits to relieve ourselves. We were also oftentimes greatly annoyed with a kind of fly, which, in the Indian tongue, is called tequani; and the Spaniards call them musketas. There are also in the said country a number of other kind of flies, but none so noisome as these tequanies be. You shall hardly see them, they be so small: for they are scarce so big as a gnat. They will suck one's blood marvellously, and if you kill them while they are sucking they are so venomous that the place will swell extremely, even as one that is stung with a wasp or bee. But if you let them suck their fill, and to go away of themselves, then they do you no other hurt, but leave behind them a red spot somewhat bigger than a flea biting. At the first we were terribly troubled with these kind of flies, not knowing their qualities; and resistance we could make none against them, being naked. As for cold, we feared not any: the country there is always so warm.

And as we travelled thus for the space of ten or twelve days, our captain did oftentimes cause certain to go up into the tops of high trees, to see if they could descry any town or place of inhabitants, but they could not perceive any, and using often the same order to climb up into high trees, at the length they descried a great river, that fell from the north-west into the main sea; and presently after we heard an harquebuse shot off, which did greatly encourage us, for thereby we knew that we were near to some Christians, and did therefore hope shortly to find some succour and comfort; and within the space of one hour after, as we travelled, we heard a cock crow, which was also no small joy unto us; and so we came to the north side of the river of Panuco, where the Spaniards have certain salines, at which place it was that the harquebuse was shot off which before we heard; to which place we went not directly, but, missing thereof, we left it about a bow-shot upon our left hand. Of this river we drank very greedily, for we had not met with any water in six days before; and, as we were here by the river's side, resting ourselves, and longing to come to the place where the cock did crow and where the harquebuse was shot off, we perceived many Spaniards upon the other side of the river riding up and down on horseback, and they, perceiving us, did suppose that we had been of the Indians, their bordering enemies, the Chichemici. The river was not more than half a bow-shot across, and presently one of the Spaniards took an Indian boat, called a canoa, and so came over, being rowed by two Indians; and, having taken the view of us, did presently row over back again to the Spaniards, who without any delay made out about the number of twenty horsemen, and embarking themselves in the canoas, they led their horses by the reins, swimming over after them; and being come over to that side of the river where we were, they saddled their horses, and being mounted upon them, with their lances charged, they came very fiercely running at us. Our captain, Anthony Goddard, seeing them come in that order, did persuade us to submit and yield ourselves unto them, for being naked, as we at this time were, and without weapon, we could not make any resistance—whose bidding we obeyed; and upon the yielding of ourselves, they perceived us to be Christians, and did call for more canoas, and carried us over by four and four in a boat; and being come on the other side, they understanding by our captain how long we had been without meat, imparted between two and two a loaf of bread made of that country wheat, which the Spaniards called maize, of the bigness of one of our halfpenny loaves, which bread is named in the Indian tongue *clashacally*. This bread was very sweet and pleasant to us, for we had not eaten any for a long time before; and what is it that hunger doth not make to have a savoury and delicate taste? Having thus imparted the bread amongst us, those which were men they sent afore to the town, having also many Indians, inhabitants of that place, to guard them. They which were young, as boys, and some such also as were feeble, they took up upon their horses behind them, and so carried us to the town where they dwelt, which was distant very near a mile from the place where we came over.

This town is well situated, and well replenished with all kinds of fruits, as pomegranates, oranges, lemons, apricots, and peaches, and sundry others, and is inhabited by a great number of tame Indians, or Mexicans, and had in it also at that time about the number of two hundred Spaniards, men, women, and children, besides negroes. Of their salines, which lie upon the west side of the river, more than a mile distant from thence, they make a great profit, for it is an excellent good merchandise there. The Indians do buy much thereof, and carry it up into the country, and there sell it to their own country people, in doubling the price. Also, much of the salt made in this place is transported from thence by sea to sundry other places, as to Cuba, St. John de Ullua, and the other ports of Tamiago, and Tamachos, which are two barred havens west and by south above threescore leagues from St. John de Ullua. When we were all come to the town, the governor there showed himself very severe unto us, and threatened to hang us all; and then he demanded what money we had, which in truth was very little, for the Indians which we first met withal had in a manner taken all from us, and of that which they left the Spaniards which brought us over took away a good part also; howbeit, from Anthony Goddard the governor here had a chain of gold, which was given unto him at Cartagena by the governor there, and from others he had some small store of money; so that we accounted that amongst us all he had the number of five hundred pezoes, besides the chain of gold.

And having thus satisfied himself, when he had taken all that we had, he caused us to be put into a little house, much like a hog sty, where we were almost smothered; and before we were thus shut up into that little cote, they gave us some of the country wheat called maize sodden, which they feed their hogs withal. But many of our men which had been hurt by the Indians at our first coming on land, whose wounds were very sore and grievous, desired to have the help of their surgeons to cure their wounds. The governor, and most of them all, answered, that we should have none other surgeon but the hangman, which should sufficiently heal us of all our griefs; and they, thus reviling us, and calling us English dogs and Lutheran heretics, we remained the space of three days in this miserable state, not knowing what should become of us, waiting every hour to be bereaved of our lives.

THE FOURTH CHAPTER.

Wherein is showed how we were used in Panuco, and in what fear of death we were there, and how we were carried to Mexico to the Viceroy, and of our imprisonment there and at Tescuco, with the courtesies and cruelties we received during that time, and how in the end we were by proclamation given to serve as slaves to sundry gentlemen Spaniards.

UPON the fourth day after our coming thither, and there remaining in a perplexity, looking every hour when we should suffer death, there came a great number of Indians and Spaniards armed to fetch us out of the house, and amongst them we espied one that brought a great many new halters, at the sight whereof we were greatly amazed, and made no other account but that we should presently have suffered death; and so, crying and calling to God for mercy and for forgiveness of our sins, we prepared ourselves to die; yet in the end, as the sequel showed, their meaning was not so; for when we were come out of the house, with those halters they bound our arms behind us, and so coupling us two and two together, they commanded us to march on through the town, and so along the country from place to place toward the city of Mexico, which is distant from Panuco west and by south the space of threescore leagues, having only but two Spaniards to conduct us, they being accompanied with a great number of Indians, warding on either side with bows and arrows, lest we should escape from them. And travelling in this order, upon the second day, at night, we came unto a town which the Indians call Nohele, and the Spaniards call it Santa Maria, in which town there is a house of White Friars, which did very courteously use us, and gave us hot meat, as mutton and broth, and garments also to cover ourselves withal, made of white baize. We fed very greedily of the meat and of the Indian fruit, called *nochole*, which fruit is long and small, much like in fashion to a little cucumber. Our greedy feeding caused us to fall sick of hot burning agues; and here at this place one Thomas Baker, one of our men, died of a hurt, for he had been before shot with an arrow into the throat at the first encounter.

The next morrow, about ten of the clock, we departed from thence, bound two and two together, and guarded as before, and so travelled on our way toward Mexico, till we came to a town within forty leagues of Mexico named Mesticlan, where is a house of Black Friars, and in this town there are about the number of three hundred Spaniards, both men, women, and children. The friars sent us meat from the house ready dressed, and the friars and men and women used us very courteously, and gave us some shirts and other such things as we lacked. Here our men were very sick of their agues, and with eating of another fruit, called in the Indian tongue, *Guiaccos,* which fruit did bind us sore. The next morning we departed from thence with our two Spaniards and Indian guard as aforesaid. Of these two Spaniards the one was an aged man, who all the way did very courteously entreat us, and would carefully go before to provide for us both meat and things necessary to the uttermost of his power. The other was a young man, who all the way travelled with us, and never departed from us, who was a very cruel caitiff, and he carried a javelin in his hand, and sometimes when as our men with very feebleness and faintness were not able to go so fast as he required them, he would take his javelin in both his hands and strike them with the same between the neck and the shoulders so violently that he would strike them down, then would he cry and say: "*Marches, marches, Engleses perros, Luterianos, enemicos de Dios;*" which is as much to say in English, "March, march on you English dogs, Lutherans, enemies to God." And the next day we came to a town called Pachuca, and there are two places of that name, as this town of Pachuca, and the mines of Pachuca, which are mines of silver, and are about six leagues distant from this town of Pachuca towards the north-west.

Here at this town the good old man our governor suffered us to stay two days and two nights, having compassion of our sick and weak men, full sore against the mind of the young man his companion. From thence we took our journey, and travelled four or five days by little villages and *Stantias*, which are farms or dairy houses of the Spaniards, and ever as we had need the good old man would still provide us sufficient of meats, fruits, and water to sustain us. At the end of which five days we came to a town within five leagues of Mexico, which is called Quoghliclan, where we also stayed one whole day and two nights, where was a fair house of Grey Friars, howbeit, we saw none of them. Here we were told by the Spaniards in the town that we had not more than fifteen English miles from thence to Mexico, whereof we were all very joyful and glad, hoping that when we came thither we should either be relieved and set free out of bonds, or else be quickly despatched out of our lives; for seeing ourselves thus carried bound from place to place, although some used us courteously, yet could we never joy nor be merry till we might perceive ourselves set free from that bondage, either by death or otherwise.

The next morning we departed from thence on our journey towards Mexico, and so travelled till we came within two leagues of it, where there was built by the Spaniards a very fair church, called Our Lady Church, in which there is an image of Our Lady of silver and gilt, being as high and as large as a tall woman, in which church, and before this image, there are as many lamps of silver as there be days in the year, which upon high days are all lighted. Whensoever any Spaniards pass by this church, although they be on horseback, they will alight and come into the church, and kneel before this image, and pray to Our Lady to defend them from all evil; so that whether he be horseman or footman he will not pass by, but first go into the church and pray as aforesaid, which if they do not, they think and believe that they shall never prosper, which image they call in the Spanish tongue Nostra Signora de Guadaloupe. At this place there are certain cold baths, which arise, springing up as though the water did seethe, the water whereof is somewhat brackish in taste, but very good for any that have any sore or wound to wash themselves therewith, for as they say, it healeth many; and every year once upon Our Lady

Day, the people used to repair thither to offer and to pray in that church before the image, and they say that Our Lady of Guadaloupe doth work a number of miracles. About this church there is not any town of Spaniards that is inhabited, but certain Indians do dwell there in houses of their own country building.

Here we were met by a great number of Spaniards on horseback, which came from Mexico to see us, both gentlemen and men of occupations, and they came as people to see a wonder; we were still called upon to march on, and so about four of the clock in the afternoon of the said day, we entered into the city of Mexico by the way or street called La Calia Sancta Catherina; and we stayed not in any place till we came to the house or palace of the Viceroy, Don Martin Henriques, which standeth in the middest of the city, hard by the market place called La Placa dell Marquese. We had not stayed any long time at this place, but there was brought us by the Spaniards from the market place great store of meat, sufficient to have satisfied five times so many as we were; some also gave us hats, and some gave us money; in which place we stayed for the space of two hours, and from thence we were conveyed by water into large canoas to a hospital, where certain of our men were lodged, which were taken before the fight at St. John de Ullua. We should have gone to Our Lady's Hospital, but that there were also so many of our men taken before at that fight that there was no room for us. After our coming thither, many of the company that came with me from Panuco died within the space of fourteen days; soon after which time we were taken forth from that place and put all together into Our Lady's Hospital, in which place we were courteously used, and visited oftentimes by virtuous gentlemen and gentlewomen of the city, who brought us divers things to comfort us withal, as succats and marmalades and such other things, and would also many times give us many things, and that very liberally. In which hospital we remained for the space of six months, until we were all whole and sound of body, and then we were appointed by the Viceroy to be carried unto the town of Tescuco, which is distant from Mexico south-west eight leagues; in which town there are certain houses of correction and punishment for ill people called *obraches*, like to Bridewell here in London; in which place divers Indians are sold for slaves, some for ten years and some for twelve. It was no small grief unto us when we understood that we should be carried thither, and to be used as slaves; we had rather be put to death, howbeit there was no remedy, but we were carried to the prison of Tescuco, where we were not put to any labour, but were very straightly kept and almost famished, yet by the good providence of our merciful God, we happened there to meet with one Robert Sweeting, who was the son of an Englishman born of a Spanish woman; this man could speak very good English, and by his means we were holpen very much with victuals from the Indians, as mutton, hens, and bread. And if we had not been so relieved we had surely perished; and yet all the provision that we had gotten that way was but slender. And continuing thus straightly kept in prison there for the space of two months, at the length we agreed amongst ourselves to break forth of prison, come of it what would, for we were minded rather to suffer death than longer to live in that miserable state.

And so having escaped out of prison, we knew not what way to fly for the safety of ourselves; the night was dark, and it rained terribly, and not having any guide, we went we knew not whither, and in the morning at the appearing of the day, we perceived ourselves to be come hard to the city of Mexico, which is four and twenty English miles from Tescuco. The day being come, we were espied by the Spaniards, and pursued, and taken, and brought before the Viceroy and head justices, who threatened to hang us for breaking of the king's prison. Yet in the end they sent us into a garden belonging to the Viceroy, and coming thither, we found there our English gentlemen which were delivered as hostages when as our General was betrayed at St. John de Ullua, as is aforesaid, and with them we also found Robert Barret, the master of the *Jesus*, in which place we remained, labouring and doing such things as we were commanded for the space of four months, having but two sheep a day allowed to suffice us all, being very near a hundred men; and for bread, we had every man two loaves a day of the quantity of one halfpenny loaf. At the end of which four months, they having removed our gentlemen hostages and the master of the *Jesus* to a prison in the Viceroy his own house, did cause it to be proclaimed, that what gentleman Spaniard soever was willing, or would have any Englishman to serve him, and be bound to keep him forthcoming to appear before the justices within one month after notice given, that they should repair to the said garden, and there take their choice; which proclamation was no sooner made but the gentlemen came and repaired to the garden amain, so that happy was he that could soonest get one of us.

THE FIFTH CHAPTER.

Wherein is showed in what good sort and how wealthily we lived with our masters until the coming of the Inquisition, when as again, our sorrows began afresh : of our imprisonment in the Holy House, and of the severe judgment and sentences given against us, and with what rigour and cruelty the same were executed.

THE gentlemen that thus took us for their servants or slaves, did new apparel us throughout, with whom we abode doing such service as they appointed us unto, which was for the most part to attend upon them at the table, and to be as their chamberlains, and to wait upon them when they went abroad, which they greatly accounted of, for in that country no Spaniard will serve one another, but they are all of them attended and served by Indians weekly, and by negroes which be their slaves during their life. In this sort we remained and served in the said city of Mexico and thereabouts for the space of a year and somewhat longer. Afterwards many of us were by our masters appointed to go to sundry of their mines where they had to do, and to be as overseers of the negroes and Indians that laboured there. In which mines many of us did profit and gain greatly; for first we were allowed three hundred pezoes a man for a year, which is three score pounds sterling, and besides that the Indians and negroes which wrought under our charge, upon our well using and entreating of them, would at times as upon Saturdays when they had left work labour for us, and blow as much silver as should be worth unto us three marks or thereabouts, every mark being worth six pezoes, and a half of their money, which nineteen pezoes and a half, is worth four livres, ten shillings of our money. Sundry weeks we did gain so much by this means besides our wages, that many of us became very rich, and were worth three thousand or four thousand pezoes, for we lived and gained thus in those mines some three or four years. As concerning those gentlemen which were delivered as hostages, and that were kept in prison in the Viceroy his house, after that we were gone from out the garden to serve sundry gentlemen as aforesaid, they remained prisoners in the said house, for the space of four months after their coming thither, at the end whereof the fleet, being ready to depart from St. John de Ullua to go for Spain, the said gentlemen were sent away into Spain with the fleet, where I have heard it credibly reported, many of them died with the cruel handling of the Spaniards in the Inquisition house, as those which have been delivered home after they had suffered the persecution of that house can more perfectly declare. Robert Barret also, master of the *Jesus*, was sent away with the fleet into Spain the next year following, whereafter he suffered persecution in the Inquisition, and at the last was condemned to be burnt, and with him three or four more of our men, of whom one was named Gregory and another John Browne, whom I knew, for they were of our general his musicians, but the names of the rest that suffered with them I know not.

Now after that six years there fully expired since our first coming into the Indies in which time we had been imprisoned and served in the said countries, as is before truly declared in the year of our Lord one thousand five hundred and seventy four, the Inquisition began to be established in the Indies very much against the minds of many of the Spaniards themselves, for never until this time since their first conquering and planting in the Indies, were they subject to that bloody and cruel Inquisition. The chief Inquisitor was named Don Pedro Moya de Contreres, and John de Bouilla his companion, and John Sanchis the Fischall, and Pedro de la Rios, the Secretary, they being come and settled, and placed in a very fair house, near unto the White Friars, considering with themselves that they must make an entrance and beginning of that their most detestable Inquisition here in Mexico to the terror of the whole country, thought it best to call us that were Englishmen first in question, and so much the rather for that they had perfect knowledge and intelligence, that many of us were become very rich as hath been already declared, and therefore we were a very great booty and prey to the Inquisitors, so that now again began our sorrows afresh, for we were sent for, and sought out in all places of the country, and proclamation made upon pain of losing of goods, and excommunication that no man should hide or keep secret any Englishman or any part of their goods. By means whereof we were all soon apprehended in all places, and all our goods seized and taken for the Inquisitors' use, and so from all parts of the country we were conveyed and sent as prisoners to the city of Mexico, and there committed to prison in sundry dark dungeons where we could not see but by candlelight, and were never more than two together in one place so that we saw not one another, neither could one of us tell what was become of another. Thus we remained close imprisoned for the space of a year and a half, and others for some less time, for they came to prison ever as they were apprehended. During which time of our imprisonment at the first beginning we were often called before the Inquisitors alone, and there severely examined of our faith, and commanded to say the *pater noster*, the *Ave maria*, and the creed in Latin, which God knoweth a great number of us could not say otherwise than in the English tongue. And having the said Robert Sweeting who was our friend at Tescuco always present with them for an interpreter he made report for us in our own country speech we could say them perfectly, although not word for word as they were in Latin. Then did they proceed to demand of us upon our oaths what we did believe of the sacrament, and whether there did remain any bread or wine after the words of consecration, yea or no, and whether we did not believe that the Host of bread which the priest did hold up over his head, and the wine that was in the chalice, was the very true and perfect body and blood of our Saviour Christ, yea or no, to which if we answered not yea, then was there no way but death. Then would they demand of us what we did remember of ourselves, what opinions we had held or had been taught to hold, contrary to the same whiles we were in England; to which we for the safety of our lives were constrained to say that we never did believe, nor had been taught otherwise than as before we had said. Then would they charge us that we did not tell them the truth, that we knew to the contrary, and therefore we should call ourselves to remembrance and make them a better answer at the next time or else we should be racked and made to confess the truth whether we would or no. And so coming again before them the next time, we were still demanded of our belief whiles we were in England, and how we had been taught, and also what we thought or did know of such of our company as they did name unto us, so that we could never be free. from such demands, and at other times they would promise us that if we would tell them the truth, then should we have favour and be set at liberty, although we very well knew their fair speeches were but means to entrap us to the hazard and loss of our lives; howbeit God so mercifully wrought for us by a secret means that we had that we kept us still to our first answer, and would still say that we had told the truth unto them, and knew no more by ourselves nor any other of our fellows than as we had declared, and that for our sins and offences in England against God and our Lady, or any of His blessed saints, we were heartily sorry for the same, and did cry God mercy, and besought the Inquisitors, for God's sake, considering that we came into those countries by force of weather, and against our wills, and that never in all our lives we had either spoken or done anything contrary to their laws, that therefore they would have mercy on us, yet all this would not serve, for still from time to time we were called upon to confess, and about the space of three months, before they proceeded to their severe judgment, we were all racked, and some enforced to utter that against themselves which afterwards cost them their lives.

And thus having gotten from our own mouths matter sufficient for them to proceed in judgment against us, they caused a large scaffold to be made in the midst of the market-place in Mexico, right over against the head church, and fourteen or fifteen days before the day of their judgment, with the sound of a trumpet, and the noise of their *attabalies*, which are a kind of drums, they did assemble the people in all parts of the city, before whom it was then solemnly proclaimed that whosoever would upon such a day, repair to the market-place, they should hear the sentence of the Holy Inquisition against the English heretic Lutherans, and also see the same put in execution. Which being done, and the time approaching of this cruel judgment, the night before they came to the prison where we were, with certain officers of that holy hellish house, bringing with them certain fools' coats which they had prepared for us, being called in their language St. Benitos, which coats were made of yellow cotton and red crosses upon them, both before and behind; they were so busied in putting on their coats about us and in bringing us out into a large yard, and placing and pointing us in what order we should go to the scaffold or place of judgment upon the morrow, that they did not once suffer us to sleep all that night long.

The next morning being come, there was given to every one of us for our breakfast, a cup of wine, and a slice of bread fried in honey, and so about eight of the clock in the morning, we set forth of the prison, every man alone in his yellow coat and a rope about his neck, and a great green wax candle in his hand unlighted, having a Spaniard appointed to go upon either side of every one of us; and so marching in this order and manner towards the scaffold in the market-place, which was a bow-shot distant or thereabouts, we found a great assembly of people all the way, and such throng, that certain of the Inquisitors' officers on horseback were contrained to make way, and so coming to the scaffold we went up by a pair of stairs, and found seats ready made and prepared for us to sit down on, every man in order as he should be called to receive his judgment. We being thus set down as we were appointed, presently the Inquisitors came up another pair of stairs, and the Viceroy and all the chief justices with them. When they were set down and placed under the cloth of estate agreeing to their degrees and calling, then came up also a great number of friars, white, black, and grey, about the number of 300 persons, they being set in the places for them appointed. Then was there a solemn *Oyes* made, and silence commanded, and then presently began their severe and cruel judgment.

The first man that was called was one Roger, the chief armourer of the *Jesus*, and he had judgment to have 300 stripes on horseback, and after condemned to the galleys as a slave for ten years.

After him was called John Gray, John Browne, John Rider, John Moone, James Collier, and one Thomas Browne. These were adjudged to have 200 stripes on horseback, and after to be committed to the galleys for the space of eight years.

Then was called John Keies, and was adjudged to have 100 stripes on horseback, and condemned to serve in the galleys for the space of six years.

Then were severally called the number of

fifty-three, one after another, and every man had his several judgment, some to have 200 stripes on horseback and some 100, and some condemned for slaves to the galleys, some for six years, some for eight, and some for ten.

And then was I, Miles Phillips, called, and was adjudged to serve in a monastery for five years, without any stripes, and to wear a fool's coat or San Benito, during all that time.

Then were called John Storie, Richard Williams, David Alexander, Robert Cooke, and Horsewell, and Thomas Hull. These six were condemned to serve in monasteries without stripes, some for three years, and some for four, and to wear the San Benito during all the said time. Which being done, and it now drawing towards night, George Rivelie, Peter Momfrie, and Cornelius the Irishman were called, and had their judgment to be burnt to ashes, and so were presently sent away to the place of execution in the market-place, but a little from the scaffold, where they were quickly burnt and consumed. And as for us that had received our judgment, being sixty-eight in number, we were carried back that night to prison again, and the next day in the morning, being Good Friday, the year of our Lord, 1575, we were all brought into a court of the Inquisitors' Palace, where we found a horse in readiness for every one of our men which were condemned to have stripes, and to be committed to the galleys, which were in number sixty, and so they, being enforced to mount up on horseback, naked, from the middle upward, were carried to be showed as a spectacle for all the people to behold throughout the chief and principal streets of the city, and had the number of stripes to every one of them appointed, most cruelly laid upon their naked bodies with long whips, by sundry men appointed to be the executioners thereof, and before our men there went a couple of criers, which cried as they went, "Behold these English dogs, Lutherans, enemies to God," and all the way as they went, there were some of the Inquisitors themselves, and of the familiars of that rake-hell order, that cried to the executioners, "Strike, lay on those English heretics, Lutherans, God's enemies;" and so this horrible spectacle being showed round about the city, and they returned to the Inquisitors' House, with their backs all gore blood and swollen with great bumps. They were then taken from their horses and carried again to prison, where they remained until they were sent into Spain to the galleys, there to receive the rest of their martyrdom; and I, and the six other with me, which had judgment and were condemned among the rest to serve an apprenticeship in the monasteries, were taken presently and sent to certain religious houses appointed for the purpose.

THE SIXTH CHAPTER.

Wherein is showed how we were used in the religious houses, and that when the time was expired that we were adjudged to serve in them, there came news to Mexico of Master Francis Drake's being in the South Sea, and what preparation was made to take him; and how I, seeking to escape, was again taken and put in prison in Vera Cruz, and how again I made mine escape from thence.

I, MILES PHILLIPS, and William Lowe were appointed to the Black Friars, where I was appointed to be an overseer of Indian workmen, who wrought there in building a new church, amongst which Indians I learned their language or Mexican tongue very perfectly, and had great familiarity with many of them, whom I found to be a courteous and loving kind of people, ingenious, and of great understanding, and they hate and abhor the Spaniards with all their hearts. They have used such horrible cruelties against them, and do still keep them in such subjection and servitude, that they and the negroes also do daily lie in wait to practice their deliverance out of that thraldom and bondage that the Spaniards do keep them in.

William Lowe, he was appointed to serve the cook in the kitchen; Richard Williams and David Alexander were appointed to the Grey Friars; John Storey and Robert Cooke to the White Friars; Paul Horsewell the Secretary took to be his servant; Thomas Hull was sent to a monastery of priests, where afterward he died. Thus we served out the years that we were condemned for, with the use of our fools' coats, and we must needs confess that the friars did use us very courteously, for every one of us had his chamber, with bedding and diet, and all things clean and neat; yea, many of the Spaniards and friars themselves do utterly abhor and mislike of that cruel Inquisition, and would as they durst bewail our miseries, and comfort us the best they could, although they stood in such fear of that devilish Inquisition that they durst not let the left hand know what the right doeth.

Now after that the time was expired for which we were condemned to serve in those religious houses, we were then brought again before the Chief Inquisitor, and had all our fools' coats pulled off and hanged up in the head church, called *Ecclesia Majora*, and every man's name and judgment written thereupon with this addition — *heretic Lutheran reconciled*. And there are also all their coats hanged up which were condemned to the galleys, with their names and judgments, and underneath his coat, *heretic Lutheran reconciled*. And also the coats and names of the three that were burned, whereupon were written, *An obstinate heretic Lutheran burnt*. Then were we suffered to go up and down the country, and to place ourselves as we could, and yet not so free but that we very well knew that there was a good espial always attending us and all our actions, so that we durst not once to speak or look awry. David Alexander and Robert Cooke they returned to serve the Inquisitor, who shortly after married them both to two of his negro women; Richard Williams married a rich widow of Biskay with four thousand pezoes; Paul Horsewell is married to a *Mestiza*, as they name those whose fathers were Spaniards and their mothers Indians, and this woman which Paul Horsewell hath married is said to be the daughter of one that came in with Hernando Cortes, the Conqueror, who had with her in marriage four thousand pezoes and a fair house;

John Storie he is married to a negro woman; William Lowe had leave and licence to go into Spain, where he is now married. For mine own part I could never thoroughly settle myself to marry in that country, although many fair offers were made unto me of such as were of great ability and wealth; but I could have no liking to live in that place where I must everywhere see and know such horrible idolatry committed, and durst not once for my life speak against it; and therefore I had always a longing and desire to this my native country; and to return and serve again in the mines, where I might have gathered great riches and wealth, I very well saw that at one time or another I should fall again into the danger of that devilish Inquisition, and so be stripped of all, with loss of life also, and therefore I made my choice rather to learn to weave Groganes and Taffataes, and so compounding with a silk weaver, I bound myself for three years to serve him, and gave him one hundred and fifty pezoes to teach me the science, otherwise he would not have taught me under seven years' prenticeship, and by this means I lived the more quiet and free from suspicion.

Howbeit I should many times be charged by familiars of that devilish house, that I had a meaning to run away into England, and be an heretic Lutheran again; to whom I would answer that they had no need to suspect any such thing in me, for that they knew all very well that it was impossible for me to escape by any manner of means; yet notwithstanding I was called before the Inquisitors and demanded why I did not marry. I answered that I had bound myself at an occupation. "Well," said the Inquisitor, "I know thou meanest to run away, and therefore I charge thee here upon pain of burning as an heretic relapsed, that thou depart not out of this city, nor come near to the port of St. John de Ullua, nor to any other port;" to the which I answered that I would willingly obey. "Yea," said he, "see thou do so, and thy fellows also; they shall have the like charge."

So I remained at my science the full time and learned the art, at the end whereof there came news to Mexico that there were certain Englishmen landed with a great power at the port of Acapulco, upon the South Sea, and that they were coming to Mexico to take the spoil thereof, which wrought a marvellous great fear among them, and many of those that were rich began to shift for themselves, their wives and children; upon which hurly-burly the Viceroy caused a general muster to be made of all the Spaniards in Mexico, and there were found to the number of seven thousand and odd householders of Spaniards in the city and suburbs, and of single men unmarried the number of three thousand, and of *Mestizies*—which are counted to be the sons of Spaniards born of Indian women—twenty thousand persons; and then was Paul Horsewell and I, Miles Phillips, sent for before the Viceroy and were examined if we did know an Englishman named Francis Drake, which was brother to Captain Hawkins; to which we answered that Captain Hawkins had not any brother but one, which was a man of the age of threescore years or thereabouts, and was now governor of Plymouth in England. And then he demanded of us if we knew one Francis Drake, and we answered no.

While these things were in doing, there came news that all the Englishmen were gone; yet was there eight hundred men made out under the leading of several captains, whereof two hundred were sent to the port of St. John de Ullua, upon the North Sea, under the conduct of Don Luis Suares; two hundred were sent to Guatemala, in the South Sea, who had for their captain John Cortes; two hundred more were sent to Guatelco, a port of the South Sea, over whom went for captain Don Pedro de Roblis; and two hundred more were sent to Acapulco, the port where it was said that Captain Drake had been, and they had for captain Doctor Roblis Alcalde de Corte, with whom I, Miles Phillips, went as interpreter, having licence given by the Inquisitors. When we were come to Acapulco we found that Captain Drake was departed from thence, more than a month before we came thither. But yet our captain, Alcalde de Corte, there presently embarked himself in a small ship of threescore ton, or thereabout, having also in company with him two other small barques, and not past two hundred men in all, with whom I went as interpreter in his own ship, which, God knoweth, was but weak and ill-appointed; so that for certain, if we had met with Captain Drake, he might easily have taken us all.

We, being embarked, kept our course, and ran southward towards Panama, keeping still as nigh the shore as we could; and leaving the land upon our left hand, and having coasted thus for the space of eighteen or twenty days, and were more to the south than Guatemala, we met at last with other ships which came from Panama, of whom we were certainly informed that he was clean gone off the coast more than a month before; and so we returned back to Acapulco again, and there landed, our captain being thereunto forced, because his men were very sore sea-sick. All the while that I was at sea with them I was a glad man, for I hoped that if we met with Master Drake we should all be taken, so that then I should have been freed out of that danger and misery wherein I lived, and should return to mine own country of England again. But missing thereof, when I saw there was no remedy but that we must needs come on land again, little doth any man know the sorrow and grief that inwardly I felt, although outwardly I was constrained to make fair weather of it.

And so, being landed, the next morrow after we began our journey towards Mexico, and passed these towns of name in our way, as first the town of Tuatepec, fifty leagues from Mexico; from thence to Washaca, forty leagues from Mexico; from thence to Tepiaca, twenty-four leagues from Mexico; and from thence to Lopueblo de Los Angelos, where is a high hill which casteth out fire three times a day, which hill is eighteen leagues directly west from Mexico; from thence we went to Stapelata, eight leagues from Mexico, and there our captain and most of his men took boat and came to Mexico again, having been forth about the space of seven weeks, or thereabouts.

Our captain made report to the Viceroy what he had done, and how far he had travelled, and that for certain he was informed that Captain Drake was not to be heard of. To which the Viceroy replied and said, surely we shall have him shortly come into our hands, driven on land through necessity in some one place or other, for he, being now in these seas of Sur, it is not possible for him to get out of them again; so that if he perish not at sea, yet hunger will force him to land. And then again I was commanded by the Viceroy that I should not depart from the city of Mexico, but always be at my master's house in a readiness at an hour's warning, whensoever I should be called for. Notwithstanding that, within one month after, certain Spaniards going to Mecameca, eighteen leagues from Mexico, to send away certain hides and *cuchionelio* that they had there at their stantias, or dairy houses, and my master having leave of the secretary for me to go with them, I took my journey with them, being very well horsed and appointed; and coming thither, and passing the time there at Mecameca certain days, till we had certain intelligence that the fleet was ready to depart, I, not being more than three days' journey from the port of St. John de Ullua, thought it to be the meetest time for me to make an escape, and I was the bolder presuming upon my Spanish tongue, which I spake as naturally as any of them all, thinking with myself that when I came to St. John de Ullua I would get to be entertained as a soldier, and so go home into Spain in the same fleet; and, therefore, secretly one evening late, the moon shining fair, I conveyed myself away, and riding so for the space of two nights and two days, sometimes in, and sometimes out, resting very little all that time, upon the second day at night I came to the town of Vera Cruz, distant from the port of St. John de Ullua, where the ships rode, but only eight leagues; and here purposing to rest myself a day or two, I was no sooner alighted but within the space of one half hour after I was by ill hap arrested, and brought before justices there, being taken and suspected to be a gentleman's son of Mexico that was run away from his father. So I, being arrested and brought before the justices, there was a great hurly-burly about the matter, every man charging me that I was the son of such a man, dwelling in Mexico, which I flatly denied, affirming that I knew not the man; yet would they not believe me, but urged still upon me that I was he that they sought for, and so I was conveyed away to prison. And as I was thus going to prison, to the further increase of my grief, it chanced that at that very instant there was a poor man in the press that was come to town to sell hens, who told the justices that they did me wrong, and that in truth he knew very well that I was an Englishman, and no Spaniard. Then they demanded of him how he knew that, and threatened him that he said so for that he was my companion, and sought to convey me away from my father, so that he also was threatened to be laid in prison with me. He, for the discharge of himself, stood stiffly in it that I was an Englishman, and one of Captain Hawkins's men, and that he had known me wear the San Benito in the Black Friars at Mexico for three or four whole years together; which when they heard they forsook him, and began to examine me anew, whether that speech of his were true, yea or no; which when they perceived that I could not deny, and perceiving that I was run from Mexico, and came thither of purpose to convey myself away with the fleet, I was presently committed to prison with a sorrowful heart, often wishing myself that that man which knew me had at that time been further off. Howbeit, he in sincerity had compassion of my distressed state, thinking by his speech, and knowing of me, to have set me free from that present danger which he saw me in. Howbeit, contrary to his expectation, I was thereby brought into my extreme danger, and to the hazard of my life, yet there was no remedy but patience, perforce; and I was no sooner brought into prison but I had a great pair of bolts clapped on my legs, and thus I remained in that prison for the space of three weeks, where were also many other prisoners, which were thither committed for sundry crimes and condemned to the galleys. During which time of imprisonment there I found amongst those my prison fellows some that had known me before in Mexico, and truly they had compassion of me, and would spare of their victuals and anything else that they had to do me good, amongst whom there was one of them that told me that he understood by a secret friend of his which often came to the prison to him that I should be shortly sent back again to Mexico by waggon, so soon as the fleet was gone from St. John de Ullua for Spain.

This poor man, my prison fellow, of himself, and without any request made by me, caused his said friend, which came often unto him to the grate of the prison, to bring him wine and victuals, to buy for him two knives which had files in their backs, which files were so well made that they would serve and suffice any prisoner to file off his irons, and of those knives or files he brought one to me, and told me that he had caused it to be made for me, and let me have it at the very price it cost him, which was two pezoes, the value of eight shillings of our money, which knife when I had it I was a joyful man, and conveyed the same into the foot of my boot upon the inside of my left leg, and so within three or four days after that I had thus received my knife I was suddenly called for, and brought before the head justice, which caused those my irons with the round bolt to be stricken off, and sent to a smith in the town, where was a new pair of bolts made ready for me of another fashion, which had a broad iron bar coming between the shackles, and caused my hands to be made fast with a pair of manacles, and so was I presently laid into a waggon all alone, which was there ready to depart, with sundry other waggons to the number of sixty, towards Mexico, and they were all laden with sundry merchandise which came in the fleet out of Spain.

The waggon that I was in was foremost of all the company, and as we travelled, I being alone in the waggon, began to try if I could pluck my hands out of the manacles, and as God would, although it were somewhat painful for me, yet my hands were so slender that I could pull them out and put them in again, and ever as we went when the waggons made most noise and the men busiest, I would be working to file off my bolts, and travelling thus for the space of eight leagues from Vera Cruz we came to an high hill, at the entering up of which (as God would), one of the wheels of the waggon wherein I was brake, so that by that means the other waggons went afore, and the waggon man that had charge of me set an Indian carpenter at work to mend the wheel; and here at this place they baited at an *ostrie* that a negro woman keeps, and at this place for that the going up of the hill is very steep for the space of two leagues and better, they do always accustom to take the mules of three or four waggons and to place them all together for the drawing up of one waggon, and so to come down again and fetch up others in that order. All which came very well to pass, for as it drew towards night, when most of the waggoners were gone to draw up their waggons in this sort, I being alone, had quickly filed off my bolts, and so espying my time in the dark of the evening before they returned down the hill again, I conveyed myself into the woods there adjoining, carrying my bolts and manacles with me, and a few biscuits and two small cheeses. And being come into the woods I threw my irons into a thick bush, and then covered them with moss and other things, and then shifted for myself as I might all that night. And thus, by the good providence of Almighty God, I was freed from mine irons, all saving the collar that was about my neck, and so got my liberty the second time.

THE SEVENTH CHAPTER.

Wherein is showed how I escaped to Guatemala upon the South Sea, and from thence to the port of Cavallos, where I got passage to go into Spain, and of our arrival at the Havana and our coming to Spain, where I was again like to have been committed prisoner, and how through the great mercy of God I escaped and came home in safety into England in February, 1582.

THE next morning (daylight being come) I perceived by the sun rising what way to take to escape their hands, for when I fled I took the way into the woods upon the left hand, and having left that way that went to Mexico upon my right hand, I thought to keep my course as the woods and mountains lay still direct south as near as I could; by means whereof I was sure to convey myself far enough from that way which went to Mexico. And as I was thus going in the woods I saw many great fires made to the north not past a league from the mountain where I was, and travelling thus in my boots, with mine iron collar about my neck, and my bread and cheese, the very same forenoon I met with a company of Indians which were hunting of deer for their sustenance, to whom I spake in the Mexican tongue, and told them how that I had of a long time been kept in prison by the cruel Spaniards, and did desire them to help me file off mine iron collar, which they willingly did, rejoicing greatly with me that I was thus escaped out of the Spaniards' hands. Then I desired that I might have one of them to guide out of those desert mountains towards the south, which they also most willingly did, and so they brought me to an Indian town eight leagues distance from thence named Shalapa, where I stayed three days; for that I was somewhat sickly. At which town (with the gold that I had quilted in my doublet) I bought me an horse of one of the Indians, which cost me six pezoes, and so travelling south within the space of two leagues I happened to overtake a Grey Friar, one that I had been familiar withal in Mexico, whom then I knew to be a zealous, good man, and one that did much lament the cruelty used against us by the Inquisitors, and truly he used me very courteously; and I, having confidence in him, did indeed tell him that I was minded to adventure to see if I could get out of the said country if I could find shipping, and did therefore pray him of his aid, direction, and advice herein, which he faithfully did, not only in directing me which was my safest way to travel, but he also of himself kept me company for the space of three days, and ever as we came to the Indians' houses (who used and entertained us well), he gathered among them in money to the value of twenty pezoes, which at my departure from him he freely gave unto me.

So came I to the city of Guatemala upon the South Sea, which is distant from Mexico about 250 leagues, where I stayed six days, for that my horse was weak, and from thence I travelled still south and by east seven days' journey, passing by certain Indian towns until I came to an Indian town distant from Mexico direct south 309 leagues. And here at this town inquiring to go to the port

Cavallos in the north-east sea, it was answered that in travelling thither I should not come to any town in ten or twelve days' journey; so here I hired two Indians to be my guides, and I bought hens and bread to serve us so long time, and took with us things to kindle fire every night because of wild beasts, and to dress our meat; and every night when we rested my Indian guides would make two great fires, between the which we placed ourselves and my horse. And in the night time we should hear the lions roar, with tigers, ounces, and other beasts, and some of them we should see in the night which had eyes shining like fire. And travelling thus for the space of twelve days, we came at last to the port of Cavallos upon the east sea, distant from Guatemala south and by east 200 leagues, and from Mexico 450 or thereabouts. This is a good harbour for ships, and is without either castle or bulwark. I having despatched away my guides, went down to the haven, where I saw certain ships laden chiefly with canary wine, where I spake with one of the masters, who asked me what countryman I was, and I told him that I was born in Granada, and he said that then I was his countryman. I required him that I might pass home with him in his ship, paying for my passage; and he said yea, so that I had a safe conduct or letter testimonial to show that he might incur no danger; for, said he, "it may be that you have killed some man, or be indebted, and you would therefore run away." To that I answered that there was not any such cause.

Well, in the end we grew to a price that for 60 pezoes he would carry me into Spain. A glad man was I at this good hap, and I quickly sold my horse, and made my provision of hens and bread to serve me in my passage; and thus within two days after we set sail, and never stayed until we came to the Havana, which is distant from port de Cavallos by sea 500 leagues, where we found the whole fleet of Spain, which was bound home from the Indies. And here I was hired for a soldier, to serve in the admiral ship of the same fleet, wherein the general himself went.

There landed while I was here four ships out of Spain, being all full of soldiers and ordnance, of which number there were 200 men landed here, and four great brass pieces of ordnance, although the castle were before sufficiently provided; 200 men more were sent to Campechy, and certain ordnance; 200 to Florida with ordnance; and 100 lastly to St. John de Ullua. As for ordnance, there they have sufficient, and of the very same which was ours which we had in the *Jesus*, and those others which we had planted in the place, where the Viceroy betrayed Master Hawkins, our general, as hath been declared. The sending of those soldiers to every of those posts, and the strengthening of them, was done by commandment from the King of Spain, who wrote also by them to the general of his fleet, giving him in charge so to do, as also directing him what course he should keep in his coming home into Spain, charging him at any hand not to come nigh to the isles of Azores, but to keep his course more to the northward, advertising him withal what number and power of French ships of war and other Don Anthony had at that time at the Tercera and isles aforesaid, which the general of the fleet well considering, and what great store of riches he had to bring home with him into Spain, did in all very dutifully observe and obey; for in truth he had in his said fleet 37 sail of ships, and in every of them there was as good as 30 pipes of silver, one with another, besides great store of gold, cochineal, sugars, hides, and *Cana Fistula*, with other apothecary drugs. This our general, who was called Don Pedro de Guzman, did providently take order for, for their most strength and defence, if needs should be, to the uttermost of his power, and commanded upon pain of death that neither passenger or soldier should come aboard without his sword and harquebuse, with shot and powder, to the end that they might be the better able to encounter the fleet of Don Anthony if they should hap to meet with them, or any of them. And ever as the weather was fair, this said general would himself go aboard from one ship to another to see that every man had his full provision according to the commandment given.

Yet to speak truly what I think, two good tall ships of war would have made a foul spoil amongst them, for in all this fleet there were not any that were strong and warlike appointed, saving only the admiral and vice-admiral. And again, over and besides the weakness and ill-furnishing of the rest, they were all so deeply laden, that they had not been able (even if they had been charged) to have held out any long fight. Well, thus we set sail, and had a very ill passage home, the weather was so contrary. We kept our course in manner northeast, and brought ourselves to the height of 42 degrees of latitude, to be sure not to meet with Don Anthony his fleet, and were upon our voyage from the 4th of June until the 10th of September, and never saw land till we fell with the Arenas Gordas hard by St. Lucar.

And there was an order taken that none should go on shore until he had a licence; as for me, I was known by one in the ship, who told the master that I was an Englishman, which (as God would) was my good hap to hear; for if I had not heard it, it had cost me my life. Notwithstanding, I would not take any knowledge of it, and seemed to be merry and pleasant that we were all come so well in safety. Presently after, licence came that we should go on shore, and I pressed to be gone with the first; howbeit, the master came unto me and said, "Sirrah, you must go with me to Seville by water." I knew his meaning well enough, and that he meant there to offer me up as a sacrifice to the Holy House. For the ignorant zeal of a number of these superstitious Spaniards is such that they think that they have done God good service when they have brought a Lutheran heretic to the fire to be burnt; for so they do account of us. Well, I perceiving all this, took upon me not to suspect anything, but was still jocund and merry, howbeit I knew it stood me upon to shift for myself. And so waiting my time when the master was in his cabin asleep, I conveyed myself secretly down by the shrouds into the ship boat, and made no stay, but cut the rope wherewithal she was moored, and so by the cable hailed on shore, where I leapt on land, and let the boat go whither it would. Thus by the help of God I escaped that day, and then never stayed at St. Lucar, but went all night by the way which I had seen others take towards Seville. So that the next morning I came to Seville, and sought me out a workmaster, that I might fall to my science, which was weaving of taffaetas, and being entertained I set myself close to my work, and durst not for my life once to stir abroad, for fear of being known, and being thus at my work, within four days after I heard one of my fellows say that he heard there was great inquiry made for an Englishman that came home in the fleet. "What, an heretic Lutheran (quoth I), was it? I would to God I might know him. Surely I would present him to the Holy House." And thus I kept still within doors at my work, and feigned myself not well at ease, and that I would labour as I might to get me new clothes. And continuing thus for the space of three months, I called for my wages, and bought me all things new, different from the apparel that I did wear at sea, and yet durst not be over bold to walk abroad; and after understanding that there were certain English ships at St. Lucar, bound for England, I took a boat and went aboard one of them, and desired the master that I might have passage with him to go into England, and told him secretly that I was one of those which Captain Hawkins did set on shore in the Indies. He very courteously prayed me to have him excused, for he durst not meddle with me, and prayed me therefore to return from whence I came. Which then I perceived with a sorrowful heart, God knoweth, I took my leave of him, not without watery cheeks. And then I went to St. Mary Port, which is three leagues from St. Lucar, where I put myself to be a soldier in the King of Spain's galleys, which were bound for Majorca and coming thither in the end of the Christmas holidays I found there two English ships, the one of London, and the other of the west country, which were ready freighted, and stayed but for a fair wind. To the master of the one which was of the west country went I, and told him that I had been two years in Spain to learn the language, and that I was now desirous to go home and see my friends, for that I lacked maintenance, and so having agreed with him for my passage I took my shipping. And thus, through the providence of Almighty God, after sixteen years' absence, having sustained many and sundry great troubles and miseries, as by this discourse appeareth, I came home to this my native country in England in the year 1582, in the month of February in the ship called the *Landret*, and arrived at Poole.

Illustrated Histories
Published by CASSELL & COMPANY.

England, Cassell's History of. With upwards of 2,000 Illustrations. Ten Volumes, 9s. each. (Vols. I. and II., *New and Revised Edition*, 9s. each.)

Universal History, Cassell's. With nearly 1,000 Illustrations. Four Vols. 9s. each.

India, Cassell's History of. By JAMES GRANT. With about 400 Illustrations. Two Volumes. 9s. each.

Russo-Turkish War, Cassell's History of the. By EDMUND OLLIER. With about 500 Illustrations. Two Volumes. 9s. each.

British Battles on Land and Sea. By JAMES GRANT. With about 800 Illustrations. Four Vols. 9s. each.

Franco-German War, Cassell's History of the. With nearly 500 Illustrations. Two Volumes. 18s.

United States, Cassell's History of the. By E. OLLIER. With 600 Illustrations. Three Volumes. £1 7s.

Protestantism, The History of. By the Rev. J. A. WYLIE, LL.D. With 600 Illustrations. Three Volumes. £1 7s.

CASSELL & COMPANY, LIMITED, *Ludgate Hill, London.*

BOOKS FOR EVERY HOUSEHOL[D]
Published by Cassell & Company.

The Book of Health. A Volume upon the Scie[nce] and Preservation of Health in every condition and rel[ation] of Life. With Practical Illustrations. Cloth, 21s.; [rox]burgh, £1 5s.

Our Homes, and How to Make Them Heal[thy.] With numerous Practical Illustrations. Edited by SHI[RLEY] FORSTER MURPHY. Cloth, 15s.; roxburgh, 18s.

The Family Physician. A Manual of Dom[estic] Medicine. By Eminent Physicians and Surgeons o[f the] Principal London Hospitals. New and Revised Ed[ition.] Cloth, 21s.; roxburgh, 25s.

The Ladies' Physician. A Guide for Wome[n in] the Treatment of their Ailments. By a London Physi[cian.] *Seventh Edition.* Cloth, 6s.

The Largest, Cheapest, and Best Cookery Book.

Cassell's Dictionary of Cookery. Illustr[ated] throughout. Containing about 9,000 RECIPES and a [Guide] to the Principles of Cookery. Price 7s. 6d.

Cassell's Domestic Dictionary. Furnishing [In]formation on Several Thousand Subjects relating t[o the] Wants of Everyday Life. Illustrated. Price 7s. 6d.

Choice Dishes at Small Cost. By A. G. PA[YNE.] *Cheap Edition.* Price 1s.

A Year's Cookery. By PHYLLIS BROWNE. C[heap] Edition (18th Thousand). Cloth gilt, 3s. 6d.

Cassell's Shilling Cookery. Limp cloth, 1s.

What Girls Can Do. By PHYLLIS BROWNE. C[heap] Edition (12th Thousand). Cloth gilt, 2s. 6d.

A Handbook of Nursing for the Home and the Hospital. By CATHERINE J. WOOD. *Eighth [Edition.]* *Cheap Edition.* Price 1s. 6d.; or in cloth, 2s.

How Women May Earn a Living. By M[ERCY] GROGAN. *Cheap Edition.* Price 6d.

CASSELL & COMPANY, LIMITED, *Ludgate Hill, London*

www.ingramcontent.com/pod-product-compliance
Lightning Source LLC
Chambersburg PA
CBHW020845160426
43192CB00007B/790